The Palgrave Lacan Series

Jacques Lacan is one of the most important and influential thinkers of the 20th century. The reach of this influence continues to grow as we settle into the 21st century, the resonance of Lacan's thought arguably only beginning now to be properly felt, both in terms of its application to clinical matters and in its application to a range of human activities and interests. The Palgrave Lacan Series is a book series for the best new writing in the Lacanian field, giving voice to the leading writers of a new generation of Lacanian thought. The series will comprise original monographs and thematic, multi-authored collections. The books in the series will explore aspects of Lacan's theory from new perspectives and with original insights. There will be books focused on particular areas of or issues in clinical work. There will be books focused on applying Lacanian theory to areas and issues beyond the clinic, to matters of society, politics, the arts and culture. Each book, whatever its particular concern, will work to expand our understanding of Lacan's theory and its value in the 21st century.

Derek Hook

Whiteness at the Abyss

A Lacanian Reading of 'White Anxiety'

With Contrib. by Donald Moss and Slavoj Žižek
Foreword by Sheldon George

palgrave
macmillan

Derek Hook
Department of Psychology
Duquesne University
Pittsburgh, PA, USA

Department of Psychology
University of Pretoria
Pretoria, South Africa

Foreword by
Sheldon George
Department of Africana Studies
UMass Boston, Boston, MA, USA

Research Associate
University of Pretoria
Pretoria, South Africa

With Contrib. by
Donald Moss
New York Psychoanalytic Institute
New York, NY, USA

Slavoj Žižek
Institute for Sociology and Philosophy
University of Ljubljana
Ljubljana, Slovenia

ISSN 2946-4196 ISSN 2946-420X (electronic)
The Palgrave Lacan Series
ISBN 978-3-031-78508-5 ISBN 978-3-031-78509-2 (eBook)
https://doi.org/10.1007/978-3-031-78509-2

Cover illustration: rfwil

This Palgrave Macmillan imprint is published by the registered company Springer Nature Switzerland AG.
The registered company address is: Gewerbestrasse 11, 6330 Cham, Switzerland

Foreword: The Detumescence of Whiteness

In this study, *Whiteness at the Abyss*, Derek Hook provides a psychosocial analysis of racial whiteness that penetrates through to the deepest anxieties of the contemporary white subject. Rooting his interpretive frame in a broad array of psychoanalytic, race, and cultural thinkers, Hook explores the visible anxiety manifested in post-apartheid white South Africans over the seeming imminent demise of whiteness as a structuring concept for subjective identity. Hook's attention to South Africa allows both an exploration of his own relation to whiteness and a pioneering conceptualization of the powerful libidinal investments threatened and agitated by the prospect of a movement past race. South Africa, Hook indicates, may serve as a test case for the possibility of imagining new identities which exceed the concept of race that still centers subjectivity in our contemporary, post-colonial world.

Whiteness, of course, is a mercurial concept, a fantasy defined perhaps more by its purposes than by any stable semiotics of meaning. For the Marxists, whiteness is rooted in an economics of exploitation and servility; but whiteness also has a psychic import that is tied to the subject's desire for fullness, to their avoidance of lack and the fantasy, even, of their supremacy. As such, whiteness is a concept that adapts to its context in order to provide the most psychic bang for its socio-historical buck. As Hook warns, we must attend to historical and cultural specificity in any understanding of race, yet Hook's analysis models reflection upon ways to address the deep psychic investments in race that span across differences in time periods and geographical locations. Perhaps the most recognizable psychoanalytic study of whiteness is Kalpana Seshadri-Crook's (2000)

Desiring Whiteness, a Lacanian analysis that dates the concept of whiteness to the early 1800s with "the German investment in the notion of the proto-Aryan language" (p. 51), a notion that facilitated the concepts of a pure Aryan tongue and an Aryan race in an "intra-European rivalry for hegemony over Europe" (p. 54). Seshadri-Crook's intra-European focus, however, disconnects whiteness from blackness, tying it to the concept of the Aryan subject that one blogger in Hook's study, ironically, presents as the very proof that configurations of race can disappear (see Chap. 4). Whiteness has a deeper history than Aryanism, extending at least to the Middle Ages, when the Crusades pitted Christians against brown skin Arabs of the Middle East. The darker skin of these enemies to Christendom, as psychoanalyst Farhad Dalal (2002) argues, was presented by the Popes who promoted the Holy Wars as proof of the blackness of the Arabs' souls (pp. 150–151). But in its more recent American context, whiteness was solidified as a legislated identity after Bacon's Rebellion in 1676, an uprising of multiracial groups that catalyzed the development of legal distinctions based upon skin color. These myriad manifestations of whiteness make it difficult to track whiteness' import through only its socio-economic context. A theory of the psyche is needed.

Working from the assertion that the nightmarish fantasies of one's own subjective demise express the psychic investments of the subject, Hook condenses South African white anxiety and its psychic preoccupations in the following questions: "What must I, the white South African, do – or become – in this post-apartheid era? What, furthermore, is to become of us whites (and white Afrikaners) in this 'strange place' where we can no longer rely on the defining values and symbolic identities which we benefitted from in the era of apartheid?" (Chap. 3). These questions pinpoint anxieties over the demise of whiteness that, in recent decades, have emerged with striking insistence outside of South Africa, in America, Europe, and beyond. Tellingly, Barak Obama's American presidency from 2009 to 2017 coincided with news reports that America had passed a transition point where more babies of color were being born than white babies (Cohn, 2016), and England simultaneously moved toward a Brexit that rejected the influx of racial others into the homeland. Across different nations of the globe, white nationalists warned of an apocalyptic race war and the "great replacement" of whites. Such racial anxieties inspired a number of mass shootings and led to circulation of manifestoes by disgruntled white shooters like American Dylann Roof and the New Zealand Christchurch shooter Brenton Tarrant, who explained his actions with the simple assertion, "It's the birthrates. It's the birthrates. It's the birthrates" (cited in Davis, 2024, p. 1). If, as Hook suggests, whiteness already seems under threat in South Africa, for many whites outside of the post-Apartheid nation, that threat is spreading, and a violent defense of whiteness is most urgently needed.

Hook shows that what expresses itself as anxiety in white South Africans are often fears tied to temporality and locational positionality. Existing in the midst of a majority black population, South African whiteness clings to structures of the past while dreading change that may spur movement into the future. This dread of the future is expressed in one telling example that allows us to also specify significant differences between the South African context and what stands as perhaps the most iconic symbol of today's forms of racialized violence, the police killings that have saturated the American media. Hook finds this dread in a painting by South African artist Anton Kannemeyer, a painting which "depicts a Black domestic worker serving up the head of his dead white former master" (Chap. 3). This painting joins threads of anxiety bound to superegoic guilt over the past, desperate fear of whiteness' nonrelevance in the present, and haunting trepidation over the future demise of Afrikaners at the hands of vengeful blacks. But the painting stands in striking contrast to the images of black men with their heads in asphyxiating chokeholds that seem more common to today's American scene.

In the context of anxiety, what Kannemeyer's painting of the head on the platter calls to mind is Jacques Lacan's reading of two images reproduced in full color in his anxiety seminar: an image of Saint Agatha of Catania serving up her severed breasts on a platter and an image of Saint Lucy of Syracuse serving up her gouged-out eyes on a platter. Lacan encourages us to read the objects on the platter as deciduous objects: they are phallic objects that represent a part of the body that is always threatened by its castrated loss. For Lacan, any emergent "subjectivity is focalized in the falling-away of the phallus" (2014, p. 168). This reading is in line with Hook's interpretation of South African anxiety as tied to a dissolving of certain sustained notions of the self, a falling-away of conceptions of the magnificent tumescence of whiteness and a potential remaking of 'white' subjectivity. But if this is the case in South Africa, racial violence in the US is still tied to the arousing seduction of race. A murdering officer seems still capable of achieving some thrill of satisfaction through his deadly embrace of his suffocating victim. And beyond the US, the white shooter still targets racial others in apprehension of a detumescent whiteness that fails to propagate and spread its fertilizing seed. In this sense, South Africa—if only anxiously—may indeed pave the way to our understanding of an undefined future for whiteness; at very least, it may display for us what it means to no longer get off on the taking of a black head.

Boston, MA, USA Sheldon George

References

Cohn, D. (2016). *It's official: Minority babies are the majority among the nation's infants, but only just* [Press release, 23 June]. Pew Research Center. Retrieved from https://www.pewresearch.org/short-reads/2016/06/23/its-official-minority-babies-are-the-majority-among-the-nations-infants-but-only-just/

Dalal, F. (2002) *Race, Colour and the Processes of Racialization: New Perspectives from Group Analysis, Psychoanalysis and Sociology.* Routledge.

Davis, M. (2024). Violence as method: the "white replacement", "white genocide", and "Eurabia" conspiracy theories and the biopolitics of networked violence. *Ethnic and Racial Studies*, 1–21. https://doi.org/10.1080/01419870.2024.2304640

Lacan, J. (2014). *The Seminar of Jacques Lacan Book X: Anxiety* (A. R. Price, Trans.). Polity Press.

Seshadri-Crooks, K. (2000). *Desiring Whiteness: A Lacanian Analysis of Race.* Routledge.

Praise for *Whiteness at the Abyss*

"*Whiteness at the Abyss* offers an essential and singular contribution to the evolving discourse on whiteness, drawing on the rigor of psychoanalysis and the theoretical precision of Lacanian thought. Unlike the broad generalizations that often characterize whiteness studies, Hook takes a refreshingly focused approach, situating its analysis within the specific socio-historical and psychical terrain of apartheid and post-apartheid white identities. Through a nuanced exploration of white anxiety, Hook not only critiques widely accepted concepts, such as, 'white fragility', but also reveals how racial temporality and fantasies shape whiteness in profound and often troubling ways. The text's progression—from a theoretical engagement with temporality, to a deeply personal reflection on the author's lived experiences of racist attacks—adds layers of complexity to its critical interventions. Eruditely grounded in literary and cultural examples, *Whiteness at the Abyss* is a must-read for scholars of psychoanalysis, critical race studies, and anyone invested in understanding the psychic and material dynamics of race in our contemporary world."

—Jack Black, author of *The Psychosis of Race*

"Derek Hook has given us a gift, an experiment exploring the contours of the "subjective destitution" that awaits the personal and analytical scrutiny of whiteness in its various, chimerical forms—as ideology, as sociopolitical structure, as psychic occupation of the mind of both oppressor and oppressed. In doing so, Hook shows incredible vulnerability not only in examining the tensions and contradictions of whiteness writ large—no less so his own—but also in using the analysis ventured so far to examine the near "cancellation" he experienced for his work at the hands of the so-called "anti-woke" crowd. Beyond allyship or perhaps even solidarity, Hook's work suggests what a decolonial approach to whiteness might entail—the undoing of both the pleasures and vulnerabilities of whiteness as such. As he writes, a re-examination of one's ethics, having been freed from the object *petit a* around which so much of racial capitalism organizes itself."

—Daniel Gaztambide, author of *Decolonizing Psychoanalytic Technique*

"Whoever wants to understand the roots of racism will find in this timely, eye-opening book a powerful critical account of the unconscious underpinnings of current forms of whiteness. Swiftly moving from post-colonial theory and psychoanalysis to autobiography, Derek Hook transforms his personal position into a political performance leading to a serious rethinking. Hook has given us the most original decolonial intervention possible today."

—Patricia Gherovici, psychoanalyst and author of *The Puerto Rican Syndrome*

"In *Whiteness at the Abyss*, Derek Hook has produced a truly remarkable book, eminently readable, meticulously researched, and highly original, Hook manages to weave together several interconnected threads to develop a socio-psychoanalytical account of white anxiety that is unlike any other. Beautifully written, pedagogic, and sometimes earnest and confessional, this book ought to reverberate across the field and beyond, for the strength of its analytic insight, humour, and overarching importance."

—Sinan Richards, *University College Cork, Ireland*

"In *Whiteness at the Abyss*, Derek Hook movingly delivers a groundbreaking psychoanalytic critique of racism. Delving into the roots of white anxiety within post-Apartheid South Africa, his insights are profoundly influenced by his personal experiences, including receiving a torrent of hate in response to a presentation on white supremacy. By blending rigorous theoretical writing with lived experience, Hook examines the insecurities and defenses that perpetuate racial privilege and positions psychoanalysis as a crucial lens for decolonial thinking. This book invites readers to reflect on the deep-seated psychic dimensions of racial power dynamics and is essential for those exploring the intersections of race, psychoanalysis, and colonial history. It is truly Derek's strongest work yet."

—Ahmad Fuad Rahmat, author of *Decolonization and Psychoanalysis*

Contents

CHAPTER 1

Fragments from a Research History

Abstract This introductory chapter provides a fragmentary overview (an 'abbreviated history') of significant moments in the conceptualization of whiteness in the South African context. Aspects of Steve Biko and Achille Mbembe's ideas on whiteness are sketched—alongside those of Donald Moss and Sheldon George—as part of an account that blends personal narrative with a series of critical remarks on potential shortcomings of how whiteness is often invoked. I ask: what does it mean to think of whiteness not merely as a signifier, but as a *phallic* signifier? What, moreover, is the relevance of the Lacanian notion of subjective destitution when discussing whiteness? Furthermore: if we posit whiteness as effectively endless, as all-pervading, as without limit, does this not make it seemingly incontestable? Lastly, can research take the form of a bungled act?

Keywords Achille Mbembe • Steve Biko • Lacanian psychoanalysis • Post-apartheid • South Africa • Subjective destitution • Whiteness

The 'Censored Chapters' of Research

Can we meaningfully speak of the *unconscious life* of a research project? If we respond in the affirmative—which from a psychoanalytic perspective, surely, we must—then a more difficult question comes into view: how might we tell the story of the forgetting, repressions, and evasions, that

D. Hook, *Whiteness at the Abyss*, The Palgrave Lacan Series,
https://doi.org/10.1007/978-3-031-78509-2_1

inevitably accompany such an epistemic undertaking? For Lacan, the 'passion for ignorance', like the inevitability of *méconnaissance*, invariably derails the more disruptive experience of 'hitting upon the real' of truth. As such, we are likely to encounter many points of imaginary captivation, many epistemic instances of 'empty speech', in attempting to tell such a story. Yet we should not be dissuaded. Such imaginary misdirections do not capsize all possibilities of unconscious truth emerging. After all, as I would insist, the supposition that *there is knowledge to be discovered* (as embodied in the figure of the Other, the 'subject supposed to know'), sets transference in motion.

And so, the question persists: how might we speak about what has been repressed from a piece of research? How do we approach a research project that is defensively involved in its own undoing, that engenders resistance to both its own motivations and—perhaps more importantly—to what it might go on to discover? How, to paraphrase one of Lacan's descriptions of the unconscious, might we seek to restore "the chapter of… [a research] history marked by a blank or occupied by a lie", a chapter which is in effect "[a] censored chapter" (2006, p. 215)?[1] This provides an interesting way of thinking about how the *practice*—as opposed to merely the theory—of psychoanalysis might inform one's research. Yet while this sounds like an intriguing task, we should be under no illusion to the challenges ahead. If forms of resistance and erasure (blockages to the 'truth of the subject', in Lacanian terms) are an integral part of any project of research, then the most telling elements will be less the finished products of the research than its internal fault-lines, its contradictions and inconsistencies. We would need to look to the traces of what has been excised, to what has been forgotten about its origins, to the forms of transference and resistance that it has mobilized, to the fragmentary remainders of repression.

What one is most interested in—or *fantasmatically preoccupied with*—is best approached via Freud's notion of nachträglichkeit, which is to say, in the retrospective form of what one has *actually described* without meaning to, in the form of what one has disconcertingly 'succeeded' in doing, despite oneself. Research thus represents a displacement opportunity, an alternate vernacular for speaking about something other than what it purports to be focused on. And perhaps more often than we might expect, it takes the form of a bungled act.

We know that for Freud it is often in the most trivial elements of dreams that we find a link to what is most repressed in the latent dream content.

We also know, clinically, that when an analysand thinks they are changing topic, when one area of discussion is over and another has ostensibly begun, *this* is where the analyst should listen for unexpected continuities. Likewise significant: it is not what the analysand *purports to know* that the analyst should focus on; it is rather what they claim *not* to remember, the fragments of earlier history, moments in which they are shocked or surprised—these are what the analyst should prioritize.

Accordingly, we might ask: What were the more digressive—or unfinished—projects within the broader remit of a research program? What false-starts, abandoned ideas, what failures (or bungled acts) might prove, in hindsight, significant? What unexpected continuities might, after the fact, be said to unite apparently disconnected topics? How, despite—or *because of*—being neglected might various forgotten or sidelined elements of the research assume, in retrospect, an altogether different relevance? We might even ask: what was the real yet unconscious project of research that you had, unbeknownst to yourself, undertaken, what unconscious question was disguised—displaced—by actual the piece of research that you had consciously embarked upon?

While these are not questions we can pursue at length or in detail here—they are, perhaps, best left to an analytical treatment, or perhaps, to the psychoanalytically minded reader of this research—I will offer a few precursory reflections before turning to a more conventional introduction and overview of the contents of this book.

Confronting *Whiteface*

In late 2023, I came across an article on the artist Candice Breitz. Her name seemed familiar, although it took me a while to recall who she was. Breitz, like myself, grew up in apartheid South Africa and attended the University of the Witwatersand in Johannesburg in the early 1990's. Today she is a celebrated Berlin-based performance artist. Then came the surprise. Her most recent work is entitled 'Whiteface', which her website describes the work as follows:

> Breitz has collected and archived a wide range of found footage fragments that document 'white people talking about race'. Her archive includes voices … covering white perspectives … from far right propaganda to everyday racism and the posturing of 'good white people' … In Whiteface, Breitz appropriates and ventriloquizes dozens of voices drawn from this archive,

channeling them through her own white body. Wearing nothing but a white dress shirt and zombie contact lenses, the artist conjures up whiteness in a variety of its guises (https://www.candicebreitz.net/).

This sounded rather close to home. Breitz (2024) evidently shared many of my own research interests. Yet there was more was to come:

> [T]he archive observes the rising anxiety of white people as … calls to dismantle white supremacy … intensify across the globe …. [It] offers insight into the ongoing backlash … as white people struggle to come to terms with public discourse that highlights … 'white privilege,' 'white fragility,' 'white rage' and 'white guilt.' … Whiteface is a portrait of whiteness in a state of panic. As the privileged status of white people comes under increasing pressure, narratives about white extinction have multiplied across the political spectrum... Whiteface parodies the absurdity of white extinction anxiety—which … points to the delusional narcissism at the heart of the condition (https://www.candicebreitz.net/).

I read this with a jolt. "[T]he absurdity of white extinction anxiety": in these six words, Breitz had pinpointed what so many of my neglected articles, conference papers and commentary pieces over the last decade had alluded to, circulated around. In the scholarly world, the tendency is to immediately differentiate your own project from whatever threatens to eclipse the originality of what you have done. And while I did experience such an impulse—an instance, of course, of the narcissism of minor differences—I realized that Breitz's work stemmed, at least in part, from much of the same apartheid background that had clearly played an animating role in my own research. It provided an 'extimate' means by which I could revisit many of my own interests and preoccupations, an external and crystalized way of reflecting back facets of my own undeveloped work.[2] From a Lacanian standpoint this is unsurprising: what is most intimate to the subject is often only confronted in an extrusive feature of the other (that is, in their 'intimate exteriority').[3]

Breitz's work proved instructive in several ways. For a start, rather than simply denouncing whiteness or separating the 'good' from the 'bad' whites, she surveyed—and performed—a range of such voices. Her approach affirmed for me that my fundamental concern was not with denouncing or attacking whiteness. It was rather with grasping how whiteness—or, more directly, the various psychical functions (of fantasy, identification, enjoyment, etc.) that underpin whiteness and make it such a potent signifier—react, are challenged, and potentially transformed, when its structures of privilege are no longer guaranteed. Secondly, as even a brief viewing of her work demonstrates, Breitz cannot claim a position of pure externality to what she enacts. She is herself bodily involved in the miming of whiteness—she, after all, performs the piece—and she is thus, even in complicated and varying ways, implicated in what she ventriloquizes. This, as will soon become apparent, was something that applied also to my own research.

Forgotten Scholarship

The original versions of the three following chapters were written several years apart (in 2015, 2020 and 2024); the first two were stand-alone essays (on the topics of 'petrified life' and 'white anxiety'). So, while each of the chapters has a similar orientation—Freudian/Lacanian psychoanalysis applied to socio-political questions—and while it is clear, in hindsight, that they each gravitate around a central problematic, they were not conceived as a single project. There are important differences of voice, theme, and approach in each, and yet in some ways they can be treated as three successive attempts at grappling with the same overarching dilemma (the same 'real'), namely, that of a historically specific instantiation of white anxiety, of *whiteness at the abyss.*

Before I describe the approach and content of the following chapters, let me reiterate that—as intimated above in my response to Breitz's *Whiteface*—that it came as surprise to me, amidst my current research projects, to be reminded of a series of earlier—albeit more peripheral—papers that I had written on the topic of whiteness. What then were the approaches that I had adopted in this work, which I had implicitly written off? In the earliest of these papers, a Foucault-inspired article entitled 'Affecting whiteness' (Hook, 2005), I tried, via reference to the Sara Ahmed's (2004) notion of affective economies, to think of whiteness in the British context both as a kind of 'technology of affect' and as an undeclared yet unifying signifier that silently anchored libidinal investments in British patriotism. Several years later, as part of broader engagement with the history of Black Consciousness in South Africa, I applied Steve Biko's critique of whiteness to question whether acts of white anti-racist benevolence were more narcissistically self-serving than they at first appeared to be (Hook, 2011a). Biko's characterization of apartheid era South African whiteness, so central in that paper, remains strident, and is worth reiterating:

> There is such an obvious aura of immorality and naked cruelty in all that is done in the name of white people ... in South Africa whiteness has always been associated with police brutality and intimidation ... [with] general harassment ... The claim by whites of a monopoly on comfort and security has always been so exclusive that blacks see whites as the major obstacle in their progress towards peace, prosperity and a sane society. Through its association with all these negative aspects, whiteness has thus been soiled beyond recognition. At best ... blacks see whiteness as a concept that warrants being despised, hated, destroyed and replaced by an aspiration with more human content in it. (Biko, 1978, pp. 76–77)

Biko is, regrettably, seldom cited outside of the South Africa context. His critical reflections predate the trend in critical theory to invoke 'whiteness' in a unifying hegemonic manner and they anticipate later critiques such as that developed by George Yancy (2012) in the US. For these reasons, Biko's analysis deserves an important place in any genealogy of how this concept has been utilized at specific socio-historical sites of analysis.

Shifting from Black Consciousness to Lacanian social theory, I went on to write a commentary piece (Hook, 2011b)—a response to Samantha Vice's (2010) influential article 'How do I live in this strange place?'—which sought to draw out the implications of Vice's idea that white South Africans should accept and live with their shame related to the legacy apartheid injustices. In that short paper I wondered—in a discussion which proved far more prescient and personally relevant than I could have imagined at the time—what it would mean, if white identity was to be subjected to a kind of 'subjective destitution'? That is to say: what would it look like if whiteness as libidinal investment, as fantasy of cultural/racial superiority, were to be drained of its narcissism, emptied out, subjected to a kind of working-through, or—to use the Lacanian terminology—'traversed'? Looking back on this paper, it is tempting to say: *This is where the trouble really began ....*

Aporia in Conceptualizing Whiteness

So why then did this work fall by the wayside? It is tempting to say that one reason was my re-location to the United States, where, at the risk of understatement, critiques of whiteness are, in my experience, viewed with less tolerance and more aggression than elsewhere (such as in post-apartheid South Africa, as I argue in Chap. 3). Yet the theme of whiteness did continue to appear in my work, even if, upon reflection, I began to appreciate how it was often beneficial to approach this theme more obliquely (as is the case in Chap. 2). Another factor here, aside from the facets of repression and avoidance noted earlier, was the hesitancy I had started to feel in respect of how the concept of whiteness seemed increasingly to be used in rather under-defined and less than historically grounded ways. Now it is true of course that the best scholarship in the field—much of which is cited in the chapters that follow—avoids these pitfalls, and that I may, as such be accused of setting up a strawman. It is likewise true that I might be accused of being hypocritical (having myself used the concept of whiteness in a variety of ways) and/or defensive (even defensive of whiteness) in offering such remarks. These risks are worth taking, I think, and so let me briefly note a few reservations.

Let us start with a point about contextual/geographical specificity. Many scholars writing on whiteness in the United States tend to assume that whiteness in the US is, to all intents and purposes, what *whiteness simply is*. (A very nice exception to this general rule is Steve Garner's (2007) *Whiteness: An Introduction*, a text which, while leaning on the Northern American corpus, explores how whiteness manifests also in British, Irish, Caribbean and Latin American contexts). Now while there is some justification in such an assumption—structures of white privilege do exhibit an alarming number of parallels across different socio-historical and geographical sites—there are also salient differences. This is especially in respect of a context like that of post-apartheid South Africa (Steyn, 1998, 2004), where whites are in a clear minority and where the legacy of white cultural hegemony is increasingly being undercut, eroded, and overturned (see Chap. 3).

A related issue concerns what I take to be an increasing tendency toward the a-historical in how whiteness is invoked in more polemical ways. This seems related to a broader trend in social theory to move away from historical to more ontological modes of critique in relation to issues of race and anti-blackness (this is certainly the case in Afro-pessimism's prioritization of political ontology [see Sexton, 2019]).[4] It is worth noting, as an aside, that one of the historical examinations of the origins of whiteness that is routinely neglected namely, *How the Irish Became White* (2008), was written by Noel Ignatiev, who was best known, for his call to abolish the white race, a call that we will see repeated several times, albeit in differing articulations, in the pages that follow.[5]

While the lack of greater historical specificity remains a problem in many critiques and conceptualizations of whiteness, it is also true—as we know psychoanalytically—that various racist fantasies and stereotypes often have an uncanny ability to persist over generations. As such, formations of whiteness will presumably bear considerable continuities across the decades (an example of how—to draw on the vocabulary of dream interpretation—*manifest* historical instantiations of whiteness might differ while its *latent* cross-historical agendas remain much the same). The possibility to bear in mind here—and I am aware that I risk undercutting my own call for greater analytical/historical specificity here—is that whiteness is not always easily conceptually compartmentalized. "To turn Whiteness into an object of thought one must first look for a point of stillness", says Donald Moss before qualifying: "This point … does not exist. After all, Whiteness … [often] generates a volatile totality from which there is no clear exit, no clear escape" (p. 370). The point is taken. Nevertheless, I would add: to forego questions of historical context in analyses of whiteness is also, potentially, to lose sight of the fact that just as hegemonic formations of whiteness have a pre-history, a beginning, so they have a prospective end.

There is also, thirdly, a tendency to shift the terms of reference when invoking whiteness. It is not always clear, in other words, especially so in everyday critical exchanges, whether *white racial identity* is being referred to, or whether the critique targets predominantly: a sociological unit of study, such as a racialized socio-economic structure of privilege or a habitus (Bonilla-Silva et al., 2006); a historical construct, i.e. an epistemic or discursive formation (Allen, 1994); a site of potent unconscious or fantasmatic investments (George, 2016; Seshadri-Crooks, 2000); a regime of enjoyment (Hartman, 1997);[6] or, adopting a more phenomenological stance (Ahmed, 2022; Ngo, 2017), something akin to a rapacious plague-like mode of being-in-the-world (Yancy & George, forthcoming).[7] The terms of reference, in speaking of whiteness, often seem to range across these various lines of approach.

The obvious response to this critique is simple: whiteness is—depending on one's analytical vantage-point—*all of these things*, and, potentially, *all of these things simultaneously*. It is worth conceding the point: the value of such varied conceptualizations is less about their ontological veracity as such than about the inventive modes of scrutiny and analysis that they make possible. We might offer a Lacanian argument here: ontological incapacity is often indicative of a 'real', that is, of a disturbance occurring at an ontological level. In more straightforward terms: the spiraling array of differing conceptualizations of whiteness is indicative of the fact that whiteness is increasingly seen—and experienced—as pervading virtually all registers of existence. Fanon's (2008) pained and poetic lament offered in *Black Skin, White Masks*, is suggestive in this respect: "All round me the white man, above the sky tears at its navel, the earth rasps under my feet, and there is a white song, a white song. All this whiteness that burns me" (p. 86). Whiteness here seemingly takes on metaphysical qualities and refuses as such to be confined to one specified ontological domain.[8] While such an argument is perhaps characteristic of the ontological turn in much current social theory, it seems also to point to a critical shortcoming: if we posit whiteness as effectively endless, as all-pervading, as without limit, does this not make it seemingly incontestable?

I find, as such, that I am increasingly remain appreciative of approaches which do involve a clear definition of terms, which highlight the particular facet of whiteness is being examined. Let me cite as example Moss's (2021) psychoanalytic-informed conceptualization of what he calls 'Parasitic Whiteness' (which, incidentally, also highlights the multifaceted nature of the concept):

> I will capitalize Whiteness to signify Parasitic Whiteness—an acquired multidimensional condition: (1) a way of being, (2) a mode of identity, (3) a way of knowing and sorting the objects constituting one's human surround. Whiteness should not be confused with lowercase *whiteness*, a commonly used signifier of racial identity. (Moss, 2021, p. 356)

One benefit of defining the terms of critique—of not invoking whiteness in an under-differentiated manner—is to remain cognizant of minority groupings within the overarching category of whiteness. I acknowledge, of course, that in many respects the whole point of speaking critically about whiteness is to stress that all whites, across categories of class, ethnicity, gender, religious affiliation, etc., are all in some ways beneficiaries of white privilege (Biko, 1978). Hence W.E.B. Du Bois' (1935) famous remarks on why white workers in the South of the U.S. failed to find solidarity with Black workers: "white ... laborers, while they received a low wage ... were compensated in part by a sort of public and psychological wage" (p. 700). I likewise acknowledge that this is the type of objection that conservative opponents use as a means of invalidating all critical appeals to whiteness—as such there are limits to introducing this as a cautionary note. And yet, when appeals to whiteness prevent us from detecting other forms of bigotry, then this surely must register as a problem? As my colleague Benjamin Strosberg (2023) has argued in respect of antisemitism: "The idea of universal inclusion into privilege and Whiteness also contributes to contemporary forms of antisemitism which exclude Jewish particularity, culture [and] diversity ... from discussion" (p. 52).

Psychoanalytically Inflected Theorizations of Whiteness

Achille Mbembe is the pre-eminent social theorist of coloniality and race in contemporary South Africa. Given that he has offered a series of formulations of whiteness, it is important—despite the controversy stoked by some of his remarks—to note his contributions.[9] In a (2015) article on the state of South African political life, Mbembe commented on the need to demythologize whiteness in the post-apartheid milieu:

> [M]any lives were destroyed in the name of whiteness... the structural repetition of past sufferings in the present is beyond any reasonable doubt. Whiteness ... [is] a necrophiliac power structure and a primary shaper of a global system of unequal redistribution of life chances ... But to properly engineer its death—and thus the end of the nightmare it has been for a large portion of humanity—we urgently need to demythologize it. If we fail to properly mythologize whiteness, whiteness ... will end up claiming us. (Mbembe, 2015)

Mbembe's above characterization of whiteness as "a necrophiliac power structure" has much in common with other conceptualizations—such as we find in the literature on Afropessimism—that highlights whiteness as terror, as perverse, as violence, as death-bringing (Warren, 2018; Wilderson, 2020). And yet Mbembe clearly breaks ranks with many critical conceptualizations in suggesting that whiteness might function—paradoxically—as a libidinal investment, an "erotogenic object", not only for whites, but also for those upon whom its lethal excesses are directed:

> [F]or whiteness to properly operate its destructive force ... it needs to capture its victim's imagination ... As a poisonous fiction that passes for a fact, whiteness seeks to institutionalize itself as an event by any means necessary. This it does by colonizing the entire realms of desire and the imagination ... To puncture and deflate the fictions of whiteness will require ... a different regime of desire, new approaches in the constitution of material, aesthetic and symbolic capital. (Mbembe, 2015)

It is not hard to see why many were angered by these remarks. Yet there is something Fanonian about them, even indeed, a quality of Black Consciousness critique, insofar as they warn us about the inherent risks of monumentalizing whiteness as an eternal and incontestable edifice that continues, despite—or because of—intensive critique, to implicitly provide the co-ordinates of cultural value and desirability.

If we were to draw on a relevant Lacanian concept here, we might suggest that whiteness has often functioned not merely as a potent signifier—and a master signifier, as Seshadri-Crooks (2000) memorably argued in her own Lacanian analysis—but also as a phallic signifier. That is to say: if whiteness as a signifier is phallic—has, in other words, come to stand for the 'fullness of being', for potency, power, permanence, etc.—then we do well to remember that any such aspiration is necessarily corrupt, underwritten by falsity. As Jacqueline Rose stresses "the status of the phallus is a fraud ... [t]he phallus can only take up its place by indicating the precariousness of any identity assumed by the subject on the basis of its token" (1985 p. 40). This gives us the opportunity to highlight Sheldon George's (2016) important psychoanalytic conceptualizations in this area.[10]

George is concerned with the US context, with the history of slavery, and, more precisely, with how "the master signifier, whiteness, and its accompanying discourses of race are rooted in slavery" (2016, p. 24). What slavery made possible, for whites, was a type of repatriation of lost being or wholeness; the embodied slave "buttressed the master's fantasies of being" (p. 24). To grasp this argument, one needs to appreciate that for Lacanian psychoanalysis all speaking beings have needed to sacrifice a sense of wholeness, that is, to give up a form of primal enjoyment or *jouissance* (this is what, in Freudian, terms we would refer to as castration). What was afforded whites, and white slaveholders particularly, during the historical period of slavery was a means of fantasmatically restoring this lost being via the ownership of enslaved people who were, psychically, a kind of replacement for sacrificed *jouissance*. In George's own words:

> [W]hite slaveholding Americans not only sought to transform the slave from subject into commodity but also shored up white fantasies of being, employing slaves themselves as signifiers of this being; indeed white Americans were able to purchase and display their illusory being through the very procurement of slaves. (2016, p. 25)

And so, while whiteness thus certainly achieved a formidable "discursive dominance as the representative of being" (p. 25), this status remained—like any such phallic attribute—in a significant sense, illusory, which is to say premised on imaginary belief or desire, *fantasmatic*, which is not in any way to deny or minimize the regimes of violence, brutality, and dehumanization that, in the historical era of slavery and beyond, its representatives have brought about.[11]

This connects interestingly with facets of Mbembe's later comments on whiteness. In his landmark (2017) *Critique of Black Reason*, Mbembe again makes strategic recourse to psychoanalytic terminology in qualifying how he thinks we need approach whiteness. There are, in his view, several crucial historical determinants that explain the power of "the fantasy of Whiteness", the first of which is the factor of belief:

> [F]ar from being spontaneous, [this] belief was cultivated, nourished, reproduced, and disseminated by a set of theological, cultural, political, economic, and institutional mechanisms … In several regions of the world, a great deal of work went into transforming Whiteness into a dogma and a habitus. Such was … the case in … countries with slavery … [and in] settler colonies … [and wherever] racial segregation became a semiotic that was simultaneously a right, a faith, and a doctrine, any transgression of which could result in a range of punishments, including death. (Mbembe, 2017, p. 45)

There is much of value here. Mbembe's alloys a psychological factor (belief) to a Foucauldian array of concerns (institutional mechanisms, material practices, epistemic formations) and does so by, in addition, pinpointing both crucial events in the history of anti-blackness and their impact on the legal fabric of the societies concerned. He continues, adding to the psychical dimension of his analysis:

> [S]uch mechanisms often functioned to transform Whiteness into common sense as well as a form of desire and fascination … [If such] a belief does not become desire and fascination … it cannot operate as an autonomous and

> internalized power ... this view ... of Whiteness involves a constellation of objects of desire and public signs of privilege that relate to body and image, language and wealth. Fantasy ... seeks to anchor itself in the real in the form of an effective social truth. In this, the fantasy of Whiteness succeeded ... it became the mark of a certain mode of Western presence in the world, a certain figure of brutality and cruelty, a singular form of predation with an unequaled capacity for the subjection and exploitation of foreign peoples. (Mbembe, 2017, p. 45)

While many would object to whiteness being understood as fantasy—notwithstanding the psychoanalytic qualification that fantasies are often more determining in their impact than ostensibly 'objective' versions of reality—Mbembe is clearly focused here on how whiteness as libidinal investment (as a form of "desire and fascination") is increasingly materialized in forms of discursive practice and bodily violence (brutality and cruelty) which stretch across historical periods and geographical regions (in exterminations, genocides, the slave trade, colonial conquests, in apartheid, in forms of structural violence). The reason I have spent so much time discussing Mbembe's work is that it is clearly inspired by Foucault's analytical priorities even while it draws on a more Fanonian, or psychoanalytically inflected, vocabulary. It both highlights historical specificity and the brute realities of racializing embodiment and physical violence, on the one hand, and the psychical register of desire, libidinal investments, erotogenic objects and fantasmatic imaginaries, on the other.

From Temporality to Anxiety to a Scene of Attack

The second chapter of this book, 'Petrified Life', takes an oblique approach to whiteness. There is good reason for this: when I set out on the study that would become this chapter I was focused on the theme of unconscious/psychic temporalities, not on whiteness as such. The research began by asking: how might we use the psychical experience of time as an index of oppressive socio-historical conditions? It was in surveying the existing literature in the field—that is, literature on the temporality of apartheid and post-apartheid eras—that I was introduced not only to John Crapanzano's (1985) *Waiting: The Whites of South Africa* but also a number Mbembe's (2008, 2013) analyses of temporalities of fixation, repetition, and nostalgia as they manifest in the post-apartheid era. The chapter takes up these ideas, draws out some of the undeveloped psychoanalytic implications of these concepts but also adds an unpublished text to the mix—a coming-of-age narrative collected as part of my work with the Apartheid Archive Research Project (Stevens et al., 2013). This text, in which a white boy discovers suggestive evidence of an act of racist violence committed by his father, enables us to grasp crucial facets of the temporality of white anxiety, including the themes of inter-generational guilt and the morbid yet repressed fear of retribution.

The third chapter does approach the topic of whiteness directly, by addressing a series of limitations of Robin DiAngelo's (2018) influential notion of white fragility. While critically valuable, this notion does not adequately conceptualize the degree or depth of white anxiety as it manifests in the post-apartheid milieu. If there is doubt as to this assertion, consider Frantz Fanon's assertion on the first page of *The Wretched of the Earth*: "the eventuality of … [decolonial] change is … experienced as a terrifying future in the consciousness of … the colonists" (2004, p. 1). The chapter refers to interview data, popular literary accounts, and to what is perhaps the crowning accomplishment of dystopian South African science-fiction, Neil Blomkamp's 2009 film *District 9*, to provide illustrations of white anxiety in (post)apartheid contexts. A Lacanian conceptualization of anxiety provides a distinctive analytical perspective on these examples, highlighting, as it does, a variety of interlocking levels of dread or anguish: (1) the bodily (or 'real') anxiety at the prospect of death, (2) the imaginary anxiety related to a failing self-image, (3) the anxiety pertaining to symbolic mediations of subjectivity and the desires of an Other and (4) the incapacitation of desire which leads to the failing of fantasy. An unexpected implication of the reading that I offer here is that beneath the racist defensiveness of much post-apartheid whiteness we can often detect an ambiguous mode of unconscious identification with racial otherness, that is, a tarrying with the possibility of being something other than what one is. In short, what feels like a type of extinction for the subject—the prospective end of a series of imaginary identifications, the demise of an ego—is often an indication that the prospect of a radical transformation is potentially on the horizon.

The fourth chapter represents a change of approach. Rather than offering analytical observations from the distanced position of a social commentator, I take up an autobiographical voice in describing and analyzing a series of attacks that I was subjected to after delivering a talk on the topic of the foregoing chapter, i.e. precisely the topic of 'white anxiety'. The contentious material—cut from a private zoom recording of my lecture and distributed widely online—focused on the notion of the 'end of whiteness', and the idea of a type of 'white suicide'. An analysis of the barrage of hate messages and threats I received yields some interesting results. The attacks worked to consolidate a form of political identity—of an oppositional, hard-right, generally White Nationalist sort—and, more than this, to stoke a politics of grievance by linking together a wide-ranging series of maligned signifiers associated with a progressive or leftist position. What was less expected was the sheer extent of the 'unreconstructed' types of racism and antisemitism that were on display. I approach these facets of the material via the trope of the 'race traitor' and by means of the idea of performative offensiveness (i.e. the demonstrative attempt to offend and intimidate by politically offensive language). Interestingly enough, despite that a great many unpleasant things were wished upon me, there was still a suggestion that I might be retrieved from the "woke indoctrination" to which I had apparently succumbed. In other words, even at the height of the campaign of hate and intimidation, I was still afforded a degree of protection, simply by being white. In retrospect, it seems evident that the talk I delivered on the theme of 'white anxiety' succeeded in eliciting precisely what it had attempted to analyze: the aggressive defensiveness of white fragility and/or white anxiety. Circling back to the opening section of this chapter: it would be hard to think of a more pertinent example of research as a bungled act, that is, of how, as a researcher, one disconcertingly 'succeeds' in verifying a facet of one's research despite oneself.

Are we any closer then to discovering the repressed aspects, the censored chapters, the fantasmatic preoccupations that might be found in the subtext—in the apparently digressive or disconnected elements—of this research? While I may not be the best person to assess this, there is clearly a type of desire to engage with whiteness at its limits, whiteness (as identity, as fantasy, as libidinal investment) taken to a point of anxious reconsideration and potential transformation. And yet, as I discuss in Chap. 4, part of what I learned in a very visceral and dread-inducing manner was that whiteness is not so easily surrendered. Despite the critical and reflexive distance one might aim to strike from whiteness, the trenchant—and profoundly psychoanalytic—lesson is: I too am that, that which I most wish to separate myself from. To apply a trenchant phrase that Lacan (1988) introduces at the beginning of his first seminar in respect of describing the point to which an analysis leads: "the endpoint of the dialectic of existential recognition, is – *You are this*" (p. 3). I noted at the outset the relevance of Freud's notion of deferred action. It is tempting thus to ask: has something been repeated here, repeated, however, with a crucial *experiential* difference? In one of the neglected publications discussed earlier, I offered the following reflections on how the topic of subjective destitution might apply to post-apartheid forms of whiteness. It seems a suitable note with which to conclude:

> Subjective destitution connotes the state ideally attained by the end of analysis whereby one has surrendered … the secret treasure of 'that in me more than me' … Lacan's [concept of] *object a*, the object cause of desire, or, differently put, that *je ne sais* quoi property which defines what is most loveable in me. To surrender this object effectively 'desubjectivizes' the subject. It means not only to have deflated one's narcissistic fantasies, but to have foregone … [the] imagined transcendence of what is most base about one's self, to accept one's status as excremental remainder … "At this stage" notes Dunand (1995), "ethical principles have to be reconsidered, since they were up until then, just another way of finding approval or love as compensation for whatever renunciations the subject had imposed upon him or herself". (Hook, 2011b, p. 502)

Acknowledgments Many thanks to all the editors and colleagues who offered input and commentary on earlier versions of the chapters included in this book. A sincere thanks also to all who offered support during the period of attacks upon me and my family—you intuitively understood the power of a message of solidarity in a time of crisis. Michael O'Loughlin and Angie Voela, who provided supportive editorial comment in *Psychoanalysis, Culture and Society* in the immediate aftermath of the attacks, were particularly proactive in expressing solidarity, as was the broader *Psychoanalysis, Culture and Society* community. Thanks to anonymous reviewers of previous versions of the chapters included here, to Nicky Falkof and Cobus van Staden for their remarks on an earlier version of Chap. 3, and to the journal editors who facilitated publication of related material. Thanks to my colleagues in the Department of Psychology at Duquesne University (especially Roger Brooke, Elizabeth Fein, Alexander Jusdanis, Marilyn Henline and Leswin Laubscher), Beth Farrow at Palgrave, to Andréa Guerra and my colleagues in the international research collective Ubuntu (for ongoing work investigating the relation psychoanalysis and decolonization), to Agon Hamza and Frank Ruda at the journal *Culture & Critique*, and also to the American Association for Psychoanalysis in Social Work and the many psychoanalytic colleagues who have offered support. I am appreciative also to Gautam Basu Thakur, Stephen Frosh, Sheldon George, Patricia Gherovici, Donald Moss, Calum Neill, Margarita Palacios, Ian Parker, Ahmad Fuad Rahmat, Sinan Richards, George Yancy, and Slavoj Žižek among many others for support and engagement. I also want to make special mention of several of my Duquesne colleagues, Anna Kreienberg and Benjamin Strosberg on the one hand, and Gabriel Walsh and the other, whose research assistance and professional advice (respectively) proved invaluable during the worst of the online attacks. The biggest thanks go to Dylan, Elliott, and Merryn Hook.

Notes

1. Interestingly, Lacan refers in the same passage to lost "archival documents", to how "the insertion of ... [an] adulterated chapter" (i.e. one akin to the dreamwork's substitution) produces distortions into "the chapters surrounding it" (2006, p. 215).
2. As I hope is obvious, this in no way detracts from the distinctiveness and originality of Breitz's work.
3. Hence Lacan's remark that "at the heart of my assent to myself, it is he who stirs me", which Jacques-Alain Miller (1994) cites and reformulates as: "the extimate of the Other is tied to the vacillation of the subject's identity to himself" (p. 77).
4. For critical reflections on this aspect of Afro-pessimism, see Okoth (2020).
5. Another important book that is rarely cited in the literature on whiteness, Theodore Allen's (1994) *The Invention of the White Race.* This is a crucial text regards the pre-history of American whiteness, examining, as it does, how, despite multiple ethnic, religious and class differences, English, Scottish, Irish and other European colonists in seventeenth Century North America gradually took on the new inclusive status of whites.
6. I draw out some of the psychoanalytic implications of Hartman's (1997) groundbreaking analysis of whiteness as enjoyment in relation to slavery in a forthcoming paper (Hook, 2025) on how the Lacanian concept of jouissance is utilized by Afro-pessimism.
7. To this proliferation of critical concepts we also need to add the notion of 'whiteliness', which refers to a series of behaviors, habits and dispositions associated with white privilege (Tate & Page, 2018), to how white people enact a type of raced being in the world which while ostensibly benign in its naturalness remains oppressive (Yancy, 2015).
8. Another crucial moment in Fanon's work should be noted: in *The Wretched of the Earth* Fanon frequently makes reference to the 'atmosphere' of colonial violence. Such a notion likewise can be said to apply to whiteness itself as a form of influence or violence that is often difficult to categorize, definitively locate or define. Several authors have adopted just such an approach (Sharpe, 2016). Importantly, though, if we are citing Fanon as a means of highlighting the ostensibly metaphysical reach of whiteness, it is also crucial to stress that race – most pertinently, in the colonial context, forms of

whiteness and blackness – is decidedly *not* ontological for Fanon (see Hudis, 2015).

9. For a summary discussion of whiteness in the South African context see Badenhorst (2020). For an overview of how the topic of whiteness has been taken up in the post-apartheid context, see West and Schmidt (2010). One of the most historically significant psychoanalytic engagements with whiteness in the South African/apartheid context is J.M. Coetzee's celebrated (1991) paper 'The mind of apartheid', which has by now received extensive commentary (see the special issue of the journal *Social Dynamics* (edited by Truscott et al. (2023) which includes a series of commentaries on Coetzee's essay).
10. For an excellent summary overview of psychoanalytic engagements with the topic of whiteness, see Truscott (2020). Truscott remarks that psychoanalysis has provided a conceptual vocabulary according to which "whiteness – in its symptomatic ambivalence, an ambivalence acted out rather than articulated reasonably, in its fragile narcissism – can be understood as having a pathological psychical organization" (p. 515). This itself is a demonstration of the value psychoanalysis brings to the examination of whiteness: the concepts of ambivalence, acting out, and narcissism all are of clear analytical relevance. Truscott goes on to add that if politically committed psychoanalytic critiques of whiteness "are not to repeat an epistemological kinship with the very problem [of whiteness] under study, this relation has to be foregrounded and worked through" (p. 519). This book aims to make a modest contribution to this objective.
11. One interesting implication of George's (2016) analysis is that white people themselves are split by or are minimally separated from whiteness-as-phallus: "This discursive supremacy of whiteness as phallic signifier of the impossible ideal, in actuality, splits whiteness away from any embodied individual who may call him – or herself white" (p. 103).

References

Ahmed, S. (2004). Affective economies. *Social Text, 22*(2), 117–139. Retrieved from https://www.muse.jhu.edu/article/55780

Ahmed, S. (2022). A Phenomenology of Whiteness. In L. Laubscher, D. Hook, & M. U. Desai (Eds.), *Fanon, Phenomenology and Psychology*. Routledge.

Allen, T. W. (1994). *The Invention of the White Race Volume 1: Racial Oppression and Social Control*. Verso.

Badenhorst, P. (2020). South Africa and Whiteness. In Z. A. Casey (Ed.), *Encyclopedia of Critical Whiteness Studies* (pp. 651–658). Brill.

Biko, S. (1978). *I Write What I Like*. Bowerdean.

Bonilla-Silva, E., Goar, C., & Embrick, D. G. (2006). When whites flock together: The social psychology of white habitus. *Critical Sociology, 32*(2–3), 229–253.

Breitz, C. (2024). *Whiteface*. Retrieved from https://www.candicebreitz.net/

Coetzee, J. M. (1991). The mind of apartheid: Geoffrey Cronjé. *Social Dynamics, 17*, 1–35.

Crapanzano, V. (1985). *Waiting: The Whites of South Africa*. Granada.

DiAngelo, R. (2018). *White Fragility*. Beacon Press.

Du Bois, W. E. B. (1935). *Black Reconstruction in America: An Essay Toward a History of the Part Which Black Folk Played in the Attempt to Reconstruct Democracy in America, 1860–1880*. Harcourt, Brace, and Co.

Dunand, A. (1995). The End of Analysis (II). In R. Feldstein, B. Fink, & M. Jaanus (Eds.), *Reading Seminar XI: Lacan's Four Fundamental Concepts of Psychoanalysis*. State University of New York Press.

Fanon, F. (2004). *The Wretched of the Earth* (R. Phlcox, Trans.). Grove.

Fanon, F. (2008). *Black Skin White Masks* (C. L. Markmann, Trans.). Pluto.

Garner, S. (2007). *Whiteness: An Introduction*. Routledge.

George, S. (2016). *Trauma and Race: A Lacanian Study of African American Racial Identity*. Baylor University Press.

Hartman, S. (1997). *Scenes of Subjection: Terror, Slavery, and Self-Making in Nineteenth-Century America*. Oxford University Press.

Hook, D. (2005). Affecting whiteness: Racism as technology of affect. *International Journal of Critical Psychology, 16*, 74–99.

Hook, D. (2011a). Retrieving Biko: A Black Consciousness critique of whiteness. *African Identities, 9*(1), 19–32.

Hook, D. (2011b). White privilege, psychoanalytic ethics and the limitations of political silence. *South African Journal of Philosophy, 30*(3), 495–502.

Hook, D. (2025). "The extensive capacities of enjoyment": Jouissance in Afro-pessimist thought. *UMBR(a)*.

Hudis, P. (2015). *Frantz Fanon: Philosopher of the Barricades*. Pluto.

Ignatiev, N. (2008). *How the Irish Became White*. Routledge.

Lacan, J. (1988). *The Seminar of Jacques Lacan, Book I: Freud's Papers on Technique, 1953–1954* (Ed.), Jacques-Alain Miller, translated with notes by John Forrester. W.W. Norton.

Lacan, J. (2006). *Écrits: The First Complete Edition in English* (B. Fink, Trans.). W.W. Norton.

Mbembe, A. (2008). Aesthetics of Superfluity. In S. Nuttall & A. Mbembe (Eds.), *Johannesburg the Elusive Metropolis*. Wits University Press.

Mbembe, A. (2013). Consumed by our lust for lost segregation. *Mail & Guardian*, 29 March to 4 April, p. 29.

Mbembe, A. (2015). The state of South African political life. 19 September. Retrieved from https://africasacountry.com/2015/09/achille-mbembe-on-the-state-of-south-african-politics/

Mbembe, A. (2017). *Critique of Black Reason*. Wits University Press.

Miller, J.-A. (1994). Extimaté. In M. Bracher, M. Alcorn, R. Corthell, & F. Massadier-Kenney (Eds.), *Lacanian Theory of Discourse: Subject, Structure and Society* (pp. 74–87). New York University Press.

Moss, D. (2021). On having Whiteness. *Journal of the American Psychoanalytical Association, 69*(2), 355–371.
Ngo, H. (2017). *The Habits of Racism: A Phenomenology of Racism and Racialized Embodiment.* Lexington.
Okoth, K. O. (2020). The flatness of blackness: Afro-Pessimism and the erasure of anti-colonial thought. *Salvage*, January 16.
Rose, J. (1985). Introduction—II. In J. Mitchell & J. Rose (Eds.), *Feminine Sexuality: Jacques Lacan and the école freudienne* (pp. 27–58). W.W. Norton.
Seshadri-Crooks, K. (2000). *Desiring Whiteness: A Lacanian Analysis of Race.* Routledge.
Sexton, J. C. (2019). Affirmations in the dark. *The Comparatist, 43*, 90–111.
Sharpe, C. (2016). *In the Wake: On Blackness and Being.* Duke University Press.
Stevens, G., Duncan, N., & Hook, D. (2013). *Race, Memory and the Apartheid Archive.* Palgrave.
Steyn, M. E. (1998). White Identity in Context in a Personal Narrative. In T. K. Nakayama & J. N. Martin (Eds.), *Whiteness: The Communication of Social Identity* (pp. 264–278). Sage.
Steyn, M. E. (2004). Rehabilitating a whiteness disgraced: Afrikaner white talk in post-apartheid South Africa. *Communications Quarterly, 52*(2), 143–169.
Strosberg, B. (2023). *Negative Psychology of Anti-Semitism: Fear of the Uncategorizable.* Unpublished PhD Dissertation, Duquesne University, Pittsburgh.
Tate, S., & Page, D. (2018). Whiteliness and institutional racism: Hiding behind (un)conscious bias. *Ethics and Education, 13*, 1–15.
Truscott, R. (2020). Psychoanalysis and Whiteness Studies. In Z. A. Casey (Ed.), *Encyclopedia of Critical Whiteness Studies* (pp. 513–520). Brill.
Truscott, R., van Bever Donker, M., & Hook, D. (2023). The unconscious and apartheid. *Social Dynamics: A Journal of African Studies, 49*(1), 1–12.
Vice, S. (2010). How do I live in this strange place? *Journal of Social Philosophy, 41*(3), 323–342.
Warren, C. L. (2018). *Ontological Terror.* Duke University Press.
West, M., & Schmidt, J. M. (2010). Whiteness studies in South Africa: A South African perspective. *English in Africa, 37*(1), 9–13.
Wilderson, F. B. (2020). *Afropessimism.* Norton.
Yancy, G. (2012). *Look, A White! Philosophical Essays on Whiteness.* Temple University Press.
Yancy, G. (2015). Introduction. In G. Yancy (Ed.), *White Self-Criticality Beyond Anti-racism: How Does It Feel to Be a White Problem* (pp. xi–xxvii). Lexington.
Yancy, G., & George, S. (forthcoming). Whiteness as plague: A dialogue between George Yancy and Sheldon George. In Mladek, K. Godley, J., & Wu, Y. (Eds.), *In the Wake of the Plague: Eros and Mourning.*

CHAPTER 2

Petrified Life

Abstract This chapter takes an oblique approach to whiteness. There is good reason for this: when I set out on the study that would become this chapter I was focused on the theme of unconscious/psychic temporalities, not on whiteness as such. It was in surveying the existing literature in the field—that is, literature on the temporal dimensions of socio-political existence in the (post)apartheid era—that I was obliged to explore a series of analyses of temporalities of fixation, repetition, and nostalgia as they manifest in the post-apartheid era. I introduce an additional text collected as part of my work with the Apartheid Archive Research Group, in which a white boy discovers evidence suggestive of an act of racist violence committed by his father. Here themes of white anxiety, inter-generational guilt and the displaced fear of retribution came to the fore.

Keywords Fixation • Inter-generational guilt • Nostalgia • Post-apartheid • Psychoanalysis • Repetition • Temporality • Waiting

Waiting, the title of Vincent Crapanzano's (1985) influential ethnography of white South Africa in the waning days of apartheid, employs a single word to characterize the distinctiveness of this historical era. That Crapanzo (1986) chooses a signifier that qualifies the *experience* of time, is telling. It suggests that the myriad social and political complexities of a

D. Hook, *Whiteness at the Abyss*, The Palgrave Lacan Series,
https://doi.org/10.1007/978-3-031-78509-2_2

given era can be encapsulated in terms of a relation to time. His analysis, along with a series of others that I draw on here, prove instructive not only inasmuch as they shed light on a particular historical and political instantiation of whiteness—a crucial objective, obviously, for this book as a whole—but also insofar as they underscore the importance of a psychosocial analysis of temporality for such a study. This, then, is how this chapter might be of value to readers who are not primarily interested in the Southern African context: as an exploration of how we might read temporality—that is, the psychical and social experience of time—as an index of prevailing antagonisms and political impasses, that characterize a given historical situation. This chapter, in other words, is an exercise in considering how paradoxes and apparent distortions of temporality—or lived time[1]—might express a variety of underlying (psycho)social contradictions. Peter Osborne gives voice to this underlying research impetus in *The Politics of Time*:

> How do the practices in which we engage structure and produce, enable and distort, different senses of time and possibility? What kinds of experience and history do they make possible or impede? Whose futures do they ensure? These are the questions to which a politics of time would attend, interrogating temporal structures about the possibilities they encode or foreclose, in specific temporal modes. (Osbourne, 1995, p. 200)

What kinds of experience are made possible by specific modes/practices of temporality: this will be an abiding concern as we continue. A related concern lies with the time of change, the temporality of transition, which might be likened to the psychoanalytic process. The time of change, as Frantz Fanon tells us, is hard to fix: always too soon or too late, simultaneously precipitate and delayed, it seems always to defy that is expected. Fanon of course begins his *Black Skin White Masks* (1952/1986) by invoking just such a sentiment in respect of revolutionary change: “The explosion will not happen today. It is too soon … or too late” (p. 7). Ackbar Abbas offers a similar formulation: history, like love, “is never on time” (2011, p. 226). The time of political change, thus understood, is conditioned by desire: it never lines up in an orderly sequential fashion but is continually subject to missing its object. It is likewise never singular. Such a juxtaposition of temporalities breeds a proliferation of *times,* the production of a heterogeneous state of polytemporality (Browne, 2014). We have a view then not only of a turbulent and often discordant order of temporality, but of multiple intersecting temporalities. We may ground this idea in a concrete experience: to pass through the various adjacent areas of any South African city is to move through not just different spaces but through multiple timelines and domains of temporal experience. Forde (2011) puts it this way: in the interregnum that has engulfed the country, there is no long one South Africa, but several, "each one a product of various pasts and presents", each of which is "tangled up in the process of trying to forge an identity somewhere between the old and the new" (p. 226). This is a case of Browne's (2014) polytemporality: a composite and internally complex form of historical time produced "through the intersection of different temporal layers and strands … combin[ing] … in distinct ways to produce particular experiences and discursive formations" (p. 31).

And yet, in contrast to what we might refer to as the heterochroneity of the post-apartheid period, there is another mode of temporality—shared by apartheid and post-apartheid eras—which, while diverse in its instantiations, is less characterized by juxtaposition and proliferation, and more so by inertia and stasis. I have in mind here a type of immobilized or arrested time. Take, for example, Rita Barnard's thoughts on global representations of South African politics:

> It has often been observed that the global imaginary tends to fix South Africa … in a kind of freeze-frame: the anti-apartheid struggle seems eternally captured in the photograph of Hector Pieterson, shot by the police in the 1976 Soweto Uprising, while Mandela often seems fixed at the moment of his release in 1990, when he first lifted his fist in a power salute to greet the crowd. (2014, p. 4)

It is this theme of arrested temporality, or, indeed, of malaise, that I want to develop in what follows, by turning to a variety of forms of temporal delay indicative of both contemporary post-apartheid and late apartheid South Africa. Doing so will yield some interesting results in terms of our broader focus on a specific, historically located form of whiteness. I start by making reference to the work of Achille Mbembe (2008, 2013) whose thoughts on repetition and nostalgia provide instances of a characteristically post-apartheid mode of temporality, namely, that of suspended history. I then discuss Crapanzano's (1985) notion of waiting. Elaborated as a means of grasping the white anxiety of the late apartheid period, Crapanzano's description of waiting allows us to conceptualize the derealized experience of a muted or deadened time. Following this, I turn to an unpublished source, a narrative component of the Apartheid Archive Project (Stevens et al., 2013). The analysis of this text—a fantasized scene of violence—enables us to sketch a form of temporal experience common to apartheid and post-apartheid experiences alike—the temporality of imagined retribution.

The critical resource I utilize in my engagement with the foregoing texts is that of Freudian/Lacanian psychoanalysis. In this respect I am following an imperative of psychosocial studies, that of isolating the psychical operations underling various social and political formations (Frosh, 2011; Saville-Young, 2011). I should note here also that the notion of temporality I apply is not simply that of lived time, but also that of *fantasmatic* time, that is, the experience of time as articulated with the unconscious.[2]

Foreclosed Futures

Mbembe (2008, 2013) provides two striking perspectives on (post)apartheid temporality. In the first (2013) instance he focusses on difficulties in respect of temporal agency, indeed, on shattered time, on the problem of radically diminished expectations of what the future might bring. In the time of political and economic oppression, he avers, the possibility of the future is arrested; the prospect of development or escape is, as it were, 'short-circuited', locked into endless cycles of repetition. Musing on how the conceptualizations offered by Fanon might be transposed onto the (post)apartheid realm, Mbembe (2013, p. 29) points out that for Fanon one of the most severe injuries suffered by victims of white supremacy is an "inability to project themselves forward in time". Thus, what is often understood as an issue of psychical and political agency is recast as a crisis of (subjective) temporality:

> Crushed by the misery of the past … historical consciousness [has] … been severely crippled … a propensity [is developed] … for compulsive repetition and a profound disbelief in … [the] capacity to shape … [one's own] future. For Fanon, repetition was the way death inhabited thought and language. (2013, p. 29)

We might augment Mbembe's account by noting that what was true for Fanon in this instance is true also for Freud (1920); the death drive is, after all, evinced in patterns of repetition compulsion (Freud's *wiederholungszwung*). What is in question then, certainly from a Freudian standpoint, is not only the disabling of subjective agency. To this dire political and historical situation must be added a further dilemma—that of how such a lack of subjective agency might itself be the outcome of an incessantly repeated type of *unconscious* agency. Freud (1920) was initially perplexed by such repetitive behaviors lying beyond the horizon of pleasure, behaviors in which the subject is complicit in condemning themselves to repeat over and over distressing situations, and doing so at the expense of any hopes of cure (hence the notion of the 'negative therapeutic reaction'). Attention to the libidinal economy of repetition explained in this Freudian way, via the notion of an unconsciously enacted compulsion to repeat, allows us to highlight an omission in Mbembe's account.

Mbembe helps us understand that the deathliness of repetition holds not only for individual psyches but for broader states of historical consciousness also. We can appreciate via Mbembe that temporality is a means through which oppression comes to be enfolded within subjectivity. Moreover: resistance to historical change may take the form of—or be consolidated by—forms of temporal experience (conscious or otherwise). Crucial as these insights are, they leave the subjective and thereby ethical dimension[3] somewhat under-developed. What remains unattended to here is the particular role of temporality in the *subjectivity of political change*.

Mbembe's comments suggest that the ongoing lack of structural change becomes tied to cyclical and self-confirming patterns in which no better future seems imaginable. Not only is it the case then that temporality is related to political agency; each repeated instance of non-change adds to an atmosphere of disaffection. *Temporality lived as stasis* starts thus to make a revised future impossible. This helps us grasp something of the subjectivization of social structure via temporality—yet an elusive but vital political question comes to the fore: how might one go about the *de-subjectivization of such structures?* Mbembe's apparent de-prioritization of individual subjectivity might be read as symptomatic of this broader problem.

Nostalgic Fixation

To Mbembe's foregoing description of the temporality of repetition, in which subjects remain tethered to the past, and are effectively *unable* to move forward, we must add a further form of temporality in which backward-reaching libidinal investments strain against the prospect of historical progress. In an earlier analysis, Mbembe (2008) invokes the lag of white nostalgic experience, discussing how dislocations of time, materialized in the forms of architectural imagination, put a hold on the temporality of progress, that is, on the time of political change. Focusing on a style of cosmetic architecture that attempts to evoke other times and places, Mbembe speaks of "a mode of erasure … accomplished against the duties to memory ritualized by the Truth and Reconciliation Commission" (2008, p. 62). The mode of effacement instantiated by such architecture relies on an escapist art of verisimilitude, as in the case of the Montecasino entertainment complex north of Johannesburg, which aims to invoke the atmosphere and feel of a rural Tuscan village. What results is a paradoxical inscription of time: "the built form has to be constructed as an empty placeholder for meanings that have been eroded … rather than remembered" (p. 62).

Such buildings manifest as signs of forgetting, of the failure of the city to assimilate the passage of time and the changes brought by it. Hence Mbembe's description of an "architecture of hysteria" that reiterates the "pathological structure and hysteria inherited from the racial city" (2008, p. 62). The Freudian allusion here is well-founded; the idea that hysterics suffer mainly from reminiscences (Freud, 1893)—that is, from blockages of unprocessed subjective history—speaks to the retroactive time evinced in such architectural forms. White nostalgia, realized here as decorative formal element, works to ward off the movement of time, to elide the pace, the reality, the *necessity* of political change:

> The architecture of hysteria in contemporary South Africa is the result of a painful, shocking encounter with a radical alterity set loose by the collapse of the racial city. Faced with the sudden estrangement from the familiar resulting from the collapse of the racial city, this architecture aims to return to the "archaic" as a way of freezing rapid changes in the temporal and political structures of the surrounding world. It is an architecture characterized by the attachment to a lost object that used to provide comfort … [I]t allows the white subject to hallucinate the presence of what has been irretrievably lost … the hallucination has its origins in a form of white nostalgia. (2008, pp. 62–63)

Mbembe aptly stresses how the post-apartheid injunction to remember is replaced with different and more comforting imperative—that of investing in a nostalgic time that (effectively) never was. What is brought to light here is the 'drag effect' of a resistant temporality in which a changing historical constellation is forever delayed. But we can go further here, by noting the fetishistic component of this architecture. The gaucheness of such attempted fixations in (with) the imaginary past is hard to deny; the factor of kitsch, that is to say, must feature as a factor in our analytic considerations. We can supplement Mbembe's characterization here by drawing on Freud's (1950) theorization of screen memories. Such memories, typically vivid in nature even if they appear focused on an apparently trivial facet of experience, are a compromise between repressed elements and defenses against them.

Part of what is so interesting about screen-memories is the amplification of formal features they present. Screen-memories entail a type of stasis: one scene within an associative train has been accentuated, made 'extra-memorable', so as to lock out a less acceptable memory or implication (Freud, 1899). Such memories are over-compensations by means of *form* for what cannot be retrieved. A similar logic holds in fetishism, where there is likewise a 'hyper-cathexis' (of the fetish object/activity) working to the ends of defense. In the screen-memory, the cathexis (libidinal investment) is realized in embellishments of formal features. The secret of the function of such nostalgic architecture thus lies in its form: its very artificiality—vulgarity, some might say—holds the clue, evinces its role as simultaneously contrivance and shield. Such architectural features are there to distract out historical attentions, to disrupt the capacity of our historical imaginations, to hold back time.[4]

What is in question here is not simply a temporary defensive maneuver, a regressive attempt merely to slow the time of transformation. The invocation of a fantasized past has ambitions of permanence, of fixity, of change forestalled indefinitely. It approximates the description Lacan (2020) gives of the cherished fantasmatic scene, which he compares to a scene in a film that has been frozen in order to prevent the next image—that of castration—from taking place.[5]

What then is the time of fantasy, and how might such a conceptualization allow us to further augment Mbembe's analysis? The time of fantasy is that of stasis. It is the temporality of fixity, of suspension, but also, one should note, of anxiety, of apprehension. A dual operation is involved here. There is the mechanism of delay, which, like the screen memory, extracts a scene from the sequence to which it belongs, thus deferring any progressive working through, effectively obstructing the flow of time. This does not mean that all of time grinds to a halt; the work of arresting movement often entails a bifurcation. The slowing of time requires the double-time of hastened labors, the need, for example, to ceaselessly repeat a scene, to rework it, constantly revise it, tinker with its details; this is the anxious work of procrastinating elaboration.

This links interestingly to the idea of fetishistic time, a mode of temporality that is both protective and reiterative, a time of endlessly repeated circuits of enjoyment, indeed, of masturbatory *jouissance*. And this seems precisely the way to develop upon Mbembe's discussion. While Mbembe stresses the factor of hysterical reticence (a pushing backward or a repression of a prospective future) he neglects to discuss a related affective component, namely that of a *loving* commitment to what was (the libidinal pull of the past). What is involved in nostalgia then is not only, as in fantasy, a type of active evasion—in this case the alterity of the present (psychoanalytically, an instance of castration), but the reiteration of profoundly loving ties to what has gone before. The fantasy, psychoanalytically, is a shield against castration, and yet also a vehicle of *jouissance*, a type of masturbatory prop, which easily enough incurs powerful affectionate bonds. We might put it this way: if, psychically, one option is frightening, then one will likely experience a 'spontaneous' affection for an option which to some degree screens out the threatening scenario. Love itself can here be considered a defensive formation. Under such circumstances, the subject of fantasy will come to experience a host of affects which have less 'essentially' to do with the loved object itself than what it enables one to avoid, bypass.

Although Mbembe (2008) does not use the word, what comes most forcibly to mind in his depiction of post-apartheid temporality, be it via traumatic history locked into cycles of repetition or through the proliferation of regressive schemas of nostalgia, is a sense of *petrification*. As we will see, this is a term that applies equally well to Crapanzano's (1985) analysis of the apartheid era.[6]

Deadened Time: The De-realized Present

In the opening pages of *Waiting*, Crapanzano (1985) shares an anecdote. One of his research participants, a man who had recently emigrated from South Africa, offered the following: "I left South Africa because I couldn't stand the waiting any longer for something, anything to happen" (1985, p. 43). This was the oft-repeated refrain that provided a degree of unity to the many stories, written accounts and personal narratives he had been collecting—*Waiting for something, anything, to happen.* The theme of immobilization, of temporal limitation is thus apparent in both Crapanzano (1985) and Mbembe (2008, 2013), despite both the varied disciplinary perspectives and the historical distance separating their respective analyses.

The waiting that Crapanzano discusses is not waiting in the most literal sense but waiting as—to drawn a term from contemporary affect theory—a general *atmosphere* (Anderson, 2009) of consternation. This was not waiting as pedantic activity, but a far more encompassing state of agitation and unease. Temporal experience here becomes a shorthand figure for a variety of anxious affects—dread, angst, guilt, a sense of being overwhelmed—none of which, in and of themselves, were enough to encapsulate the state of malaise he was struggling to articulate. The banality of waiting, the everydayness of the experience, furthermore, works well to counter-act any metaphysical or melodramatic connotations to this characterization of temporality. Waiting understood in this way—and the parallels with Mbembe are again striking—involves a kind of incapacity toward the future, and a de-realization of the present:

> Waiting means to be oriented in time in a special way. It is directed toward the future – not an expansive future, however, but a constricted one that closes in on the present. In waiting, the present is always secondary to the future. It is held in expectation … It is a sort of holding action – a lingering. (In extreme forms waiting can lead to paralysis). In waiting, the present loses its focus in the now. The world in its immediacy slips away; it is derealized … It is numb, muted, dead. It's only meaning lies in the future – in the arrival or non-arrival of the object of waiting. (Crapanzano, 1985, p. 45)

The paradoxical temporality of waiting is wonderfully described here. On the one hand waiting means that the present is very much premised upon the future; placed in parentheses by it; made subjunctive to it; even, perhaps, undermined, *virtualized* by it. Its substantiality is eroded. Yet on the other hand the immediacy of the now—Crapanzano nicely distinguishes between the generality of 'the present' and the specificity of 'the now'—is heightened, underscored by the tension between the future *as expected* and the present as thus diluted.

What is perhaps uncomfortably apparent here is the degree to which Crapanzano's characterization of late apartheid temporality chimes with that of the post-apartheid era. In both such cases, the anxious interchange of an unstable present and an unknown future seems crucial, as does a type of affective de-realization. We can bring a different analytical framework to bear here, both so as to stress an apparent omission in the Crapanzano's analysis—the past is not particularly stressed in his thoughts on the futurity of waiting—and so to further develop the factor of anxiously virtualized experience.

I have in mind here Freud's (1950) notion of deferred action (*nachträglichkeit*), that is, the psychical temporality of the retroactive which disrupts linear or chronological time. Historical events, from this perspective, remain latent, effectively incomplete, subject to the contingencies of later circumstances through which they might be reactivated in unexpected ways. The ambiguities of Freud's notion are multiple, particularly so in cases of concatenated or 'overrunning' histories such as that of the post-apartheid era. There is, firstly, the idea that the true significance of a past event will only be realized in a subsequent future, once retroactively triggered. Neither static nor consolidated then, the fragmentary residues of lingering histories themselves constitute latent modes of the present. What this ensures—a second important point—is the virtual quality of the present which, underscored by an as of yet indefinite past, remains itself precarious, open to further re-articulation. To speak of apartheid *nachträglichkeit* means then that this history has not as yet been fully resolved, that it underlies the present, conditioning what it—and its prospective futures—have *not as yet become*. We need add to this, thirdly, the prospect of the movement from the future to the past, the retroactive 'determination' of *what has been* by *what is to come*. This aspect of deferred action means that we are caught within the anxious possibility that the re-visioning of our past will necessarily change what 'we will have been'. Waiting thus is not merely an anxious state by virtue of how it relates to an indeterminate future; its anxiety is also the result of the as of yet uncertain influence of *the past* on what is yet to come.

The pertinence of the psychoanalytic notion of retroactive causality to the post-apartheid context seems immediately evident. One might contend that the simultaneity of two eras—as signified by the ambiguous contraction '(post)apartheid'—provides us with a case in point of historical *nachträglichkeit*, the sobering possibility, that is to say, of 'the post-apartheid' being viewed as apartheid's deferred action.

Waiting, is, clearly, an inclusive term, spanning an array of experiential phenomena; it is, moreover, a complex mode of temporality. Aware of the need to qualify the concept, Crapanzano appeals to a series of theoretical resources including, perhaps most importantly, psychoanalysis. The psychical dimension of waiting—and, by extrapolation, of modes of temporality more generally—is stressed when Crapanzano insists that waiting is "infused with desire" (1985, p. 26).

We can hence distinguish between waiting in its positive polarity—waiting as happily expectant state, as *longing*—from its negative polarity, in which one awaits not something desirable, but rather something dreaded. Psychoanalytically we might add that such polarities of desire represent not separate conditions, as much as different facets of a single ambivalent complex of affects. The proximity of wishfulness and the nightmarish in dreams is perhaps enough to make the point: desire and dread exist in an intertwined form. This seems to do justice to the fact that agitation features even in happily expectant states of waiting, and to the presence of disturbing forms of arousal—of *jouissance*—even in conditions of dread. This overlap of affective states is an indication that we are, once again, in the terrain of fantasy. This is not a point registered by Crapanzano, and it is linked to what I shall go on to identify as a crucial shortcoming of his account.

None of the above is to suggest that a general affective atmosphere doesn't prevail in a given populace. Moreover, a variety of adjacent (socio-economic or racially-designated) groups, each of which is affected by the same broadly suspended sense of time, may nonetheless manifest different relations to a dominant mode of temporality.[7] Crapanzano is alive to such complexities, noting that dominant and dominated alike are subjected to the affective climate installed by apartheid: "Both the dominant and the dominated are equally caught within [the system of apartheid]" (1985, p. 20). South Africa as a whole, he affirms, "is caught in a deadened time of waiting" (1985, p. xix). However:

> For most whites, waiting is compounded by fear; for most Blacks, however great their despair, waiting is illuminated by hope, by a belief that time is on their side. For coloureds [that is, mixed-race South Africans] and Asians, there is both fear and hope in waiting. (1985, p. xix)

This remark once again points to the role of temporality in the subjectivity of political change. Hence no doubt the degree to which temporality often features as such a vital feature of political rhetoric. Staying with the South African context, we might take as an example the idea, often asserted by Pan-Africanists the likes of Robert Sobukwe and proponents of Black Consciousness, that time—indeed *history*—was most definitely on their side, that historical change in South Africa was inevitable, and was—to use yet another resonant phrase—'only a matter of time'. Such a political rhetoric of temporality is itself often paradoxical, both encouraging a sense of subjective agency, and yet also locating agency in history itself.[8] Or differently put: meaningful political agency means stimulating not only a broader structural sense of temporal agency but animating also a subjective temporal imaginary alongside it—precisely what, according to Mbembe (2008, 2013) is being impeded in many post-apartheid contexts. This links us back to the terms of the foregoing discussion: one means of desubjectivizing structures, of transforming a subjective relation to oppressive structures, lies precisely in formulating an alternative temporal imaginary.

Expectancy … and Dread

Crapanzano makes sustained reference to psychoanalysis in considering the particular temporality of the oppressor, distinguishing here between phenomena of fear and anxiety. The longstanding psychoanalytic distinction is well-known: phobia has a clear object—something one is afraid of—whereas anxiety, by definition, is free-floating, cut adrift from a prospective object which cannot be located (Freud, 1926). The difference between a well-founded fear, say a clearly-defined scene of disaster, and a potentially far more disconcerting and undefined *atmosphere* of anxiety is apparent in one of Crapanzano's chief conclusions:

> [T]o wait for something that is undetermined is a terrible kind of waiting, worse … than to wait for something specific. To make waiting more specific, those who wait can postulate a symbolic object to reduce anxiety, but they risk "sacrificing 'reality' to 'psychic need'". (1985, p. 46)

Crapanzano's argument, developed via a paraphrasing of key Freudian concepts, will prove important in the narrative extract I introduce in the next section. It suffices here to flag two important ideas. Firstly, that states of anxiety may vacillate with periods of more clearly-defined phobia. Secondly, that subjects may prioritize a phobic scenario, and, more than this, that they might play their part in actively (if unconsciously) constructing just such a scene. Simply put, those who are subjected to the dread of ominous waiting may prefer to convince themselves of the terrible inevitability of a projected object of fear rather than give themselves up to an ever-undefined condition of anxiety.

The idea that Mbembe gives such forceful expression to above, the notion of subjective incapacitation as mediated by temporality, is likewise present in Crapanzano's analysis. The act of waiting taxes the imaginative and inter-subjective capacities of such subjects. They lose the ability to temporarily negate their identities, to "be imaginatively open to the complex and never very certain reality around them" (p. xix). By contrast, they close off, and "create a kind of psychological apartheid" (p. xix).

Crapanzano's speculative account is subsequently supported by a layering of empirical details pertaining particularly to the lives of apartheid's dominant class:

> The life of those white South Africans with whom I talked … impressed me as somehow truncated. I found signs of anxiety, helplessness, vulnerability, and rage that were not very far from the surface. Their experience was not open-ended, expansive, and adventurous. It did not elicit optimism and positive excitement. It was limited. Their present seemed devoid of the vitality that I associate with leading a fulfilling life. It seemed mechanical, numb, and muted …. It was infused with uncertainty or at times what appeared to me to be a compensatory overcertainty, a stubborn and harsh pragmatism. (1985, p. 44)

The indefinite delay of extended waiting produces a hardening; in the place of receptivity and 'negative capability' there is instead rigidity, indeed—to draw on the metaphor I introduced above—a *petrification*, in both prospective senses of the term.

One last aspect of Crapanzano's (1985) account is worth stressing: the factor of the missing—or difficult to locate—object of fear. We have already made the psychoanalytic qualification that anxiety is ostensibly objectless. Yet, while apparently endorsing such a qualification, Crapanzano nonetheless persists in speaking of fear rather than anxiety. This, moreover, is a paradoxical and shifting type of fear which is not what it at first appears to be, and that seems to avoid encapsulation in any definite object:

> I came to understand something about [white] South African society. Fear is pervasive…it is not…the fear of change: the loss of power, status, and wealth, "the good life" … It is, I believe, a much more primordial fear that comes from the absence of any possibility of a vital relationship with most of the people around one. It is unspoken, pervasive fear that has its source in

apartheid and that maintains apartheid in all its virulence. (Crapanzano, 1985, p. 21)

This is perhaps the least satisfying aspect of Crapanzano's analysis. True enough, he offers an articulate description of the role of fear in the libidinal economy of apartheid society, a society which can quite rightly be understood along the lines he offers, as a type of deadened and deadening life.[9] Yet while his commentary pinpoints the impasses of (inter)subjectivity ("the absence of vital relations") that surely did and that *do* characterize apartheid and post-apartheid realms respectively, it is nevertheless a conceptual dead-end to point to a type of "primordial fear" by way of a final explanation. Virtually any fear or aversive behavior could be explained away in this fashion; and such a proto-typical (or, indeed, "primordial") affect that potentially explains all fears, actually effectively explains none. An important piece of Crapanzano's conceptual puzzle remains missing.

Apartheid 'Immortality'

Thus far I have relied on existing literature to highlight a series of related modes of (post)apartheid temporality. I want now to examine an extract from a narrative contributed to the Apartheid Archive (https://www.communityidentity.com.au/portfolio/the-apartheid-archives-project/). My focus in what follows changes accordingly, from the domain of broader political and ethnographic social theorization to a more confined empirical example. My analysis will extend many of the ideas introduced above—particularly Crapanzano's (1985) notion of anxious waiting—while adding several additional components. I have selected the text not only because it resonates with many of the notions of temporality already discussed, but because it links aspects of apartheid and post-apartheid temporalities and foregrounds a type of white anxiety (the focus of Chap. 3). The text itself occupies an intermediary position: while it is of an apartheid experience, it has been recalled and reformulated in a post-apartheid era. The same is often noted of the Apartheid Archive's collection of narratives generally: while they ostensibly aim to shed light on the apartheid era, these texts are often far more revealing of the priorities and injunctions of the post-apartheid context (Eagle & Bowman, 2010).

A brief description of the Apartheid Archive Project will contextualize the narrative. The Apartheid Archive Project (AAP) (Stevens et al., 2013) was a collaborative research group that aimed to collect narrative accounts from a wide range of South Africans about their experiences of racism during apartheid. A key objective of AAP was to document the experiences of ordinary South Africans whose accounts may not otherwise have been recorded (Apartheid Archive Project, 2010). The project aimed to explore how such lingering experiences of racism, social division and racialized oppression remain important—if often unspoken—factors in the constitution of the post-apartheid present. As is noted in the project's original research document: "[apartheid's] pernicious effects on our inner-worlds; on memory, identity and subjectivity, continue to constrain the promises of a truly post-apartheid South Africa" (https://www.communityidentity.com.au/portfolio/the-apartheid-archives-project/). The agenda of the project was not only to record and collect narratives accounts, but to theoretically and analytically with the narratives (see Bowman et al., 2010; Duncan et al., 2012; Hook & Long, 2011; Stevens et al., 2013; Stevens & Laubscher, 2010).

The narrative that I discuss is notable in several respects. It very powerfully invokes a sense of suffocating or *never-moving* time, a fact rather cryptically alluded to in the given title of the piece: 'Immortality'. The narrative, furthermore, which depicts a scene in the life of a boy growing up in 1980's Johannesburg, conforms largely to the literary genre of the short story. It succeeds in conjuring up a child's sense of a white suburban household in which something is vaguely amiss. Suffice to say, I resonated with the text—it seemed to me to encapsulate something of the experience of growing up as a white child under the conditions of apartheid. Rather than cite the entire (rather lengthy) narrative, I have opted, in the following section, to summarize the story's opening scenes.

Attempting to alleviate his boredom, the young protagonist of the story finds his way into the neglected and uninhabited 'maid's room' that exists as an extension to home in which he and his parents live. The room, usually locked-up and out of bounds, has, on this occasion, been left open by his mother, and the boy wastes little time in exploring this prohibited space. He notices his mother's neglected sewing things—needles, bolts of fabric, a large pair of black scissors—but these do not hold his attention for long. He is marginally more interested in the contents of a discarded toolbox. Gradually the range of objects he unearths become more ominous, as do the memories and prohibitions associated with them. He finds an axe, a Stanley-knife, a rusted saw with a jagged blade. He recalls his father's warning that dangerous tools must always be locked away, a warning which upon reflection poses the question: 'Why?' Although he is initially reticent, sensing that he is about to break some unspoken family taboo, he peers inside a series of old packing-trunks and finds "a series of discarded African curios, a hide-covered Zulu shield, a short assegai, a knobkerrie [a kind of club] and … a policeman's truncheon, made of ebony".

What is striking up until this point in the narrative is the degree to which the story is being told through objects rather than people, via the depersonalized world of things. Also, whether the author has intended it or not, the scene of the boy's rummaging around in the dusty, neglected trunks, works perfectly to symbolize his search through the contents of the family's repressed history. Similarly noteworthy is the succession of objects, which, in the movement from the mundane and domestic to the more overtly threatening and 'negrophobic', effectively unpeels the layers of white (un)conscious preoccupation with the figure of the black intruder. What comes to the fore here is the anxious white preoccupation—something arguably exacerbated rather than diminished in the post-apartheid context—with the specter of black violence.

The last in this series of objects—the assegai, truncheon, and knobkerrie—particularly—elicit a stream of images in the boy's imagination. In the ensuing epiphany, he succeeds in piecing together fragments of a family history that had often before been hinted at, but that had never been fully revealed to him. He pictures what he takes to be a pivotal moment before he was born, a scene in which his father, who had been a policeman, aggressively assaults a black man. Let us turn directly to the text:

> The image that he attaches to the truncheon is surprisingly vivid. It is an imagined memory, of his father as a policeman, striking a black man, delivering a shattering blow to the back of the man's head. This imagining brings with it a texture, the projected sensation of what the back of this man's head would have felt like, the scratchy surface of thinly curled black hair, the opacity of the deeply pigmented skin …. He can't place the "memory"; it must be a fabrication, but so vividly is he able to picture it, so palpable the sensations, that in some or other way, it must have occurred.
>
> The tangle of suspicions, the morass of unasked questions about his family's past is now clear. The disarray of incoherent ideas and misgivings, the clutter of naïve presumptions, avoidances and fears … has now assembled into a whole truth. This is what had come before him …. His father had delivered a blow to a man's head, a blow whose consequences could not be undone …. And now he understands: they will live in a condition of suspended guilt, in a state of subliminal fear, for the reprisal that may never come.

We could read this anxious time as a variation on Crapanzano's (1985) conceptualization of waiting. Yet it would be misleading to do so; this expectant condition is different in several important respects. It is a state of unconscious expectancy for a retaliation that seems forever delayed yet. True enough, it is predicated on an awful yet unclear vision of the future, and thus shares something of the futurity emphasized by Crapanzano. It is however fundamentally anchored in the past, and it entails a dreadful sense of inevitability ("consequences [that] could not be undone"). It is, essentially, a form of dread underwritten by the forever suspended threat of retribution which has made it an immortal, unending condition. This is different to Crapanzano's notion of waiting, which stresses the de-realization of the present via an anxiety-provokingly open-ended future.

One has in the narrative a sense of the gradual advance of traumatic material. As we so often find in the clinical treatment of anxiety, a repressed traumatic nucleus is nowhere directly evident, yet its displaced presence is nonetheless apparent in a fragmentary and distributed manner, in many of the arbitrary objects and features of the surrounding domain. This is why so many of the household objects in the narrative take on an ominous quality. In such a state of repressed fear, each such object, from the tools to the African souvenirs, is a potential weapon, an instrument of violence. This time of suspension is made all the worse inasmuch as the fear—that of attack by one or more mistreated or maligned black men—is itself largely repressed, leaving an undefined anxiety in its wake.[10]

This attention to mechanisms of repression—to how fear is displaced, re-distributed, made diffuse—opens a fresh perspective on the above-noted shortcoming of Crapanzano's (1985) analysis, i.e. his characterization of the "primordial" aspect of white apartheid fear. This is what Crapanzano aims at: a description of a type of fear-in-waiting which shades in and out of anxiety; which is at the same time non-definitive and elementary; which avoids concretization in any one object. I have already argued that if we are to adequately grasp the anxious de-realization of waiting, we need to take into account the factor of the past, or, more accurately, the dimension of deferred action (Freud's *nachträglichkeit*), which destabilizes both what the present and the future might be. The foregoing textual example makes this, the factor of the *weight of the past*, abundantly clear. It benefits us, furthermore, to emphasize the role of fantasy alongside that of deferred action here; both such concepts stress the role of the subject's past as a frame of sorts—a type of suspended disposition—for how the present and the future will come to impact them. Yet this is not the only way the above text helps us add to Crapanzano's account. The complex notion of fear he describes is surely better conceptualized by exploring how it animates and deploys prevailing societal stereotypes, and, moreover, by stressing its repressed dynamic and unconscious aspects.

The repression in question is of course partial, it is—and the story illustrates this point very nicely—intermittent, continually in the process of coming undone. Emphasizing this—the fact of a never fully secure repression—gives us a sense of the mobility, the haziness, the omnipresent haunting quality of the fear that Crapanzano (1985) hoped to capture by referring to "the primordial". The uncertain relationship between fear and anxiety can likewise be illuminated in this way. When the conditions of repression are in place and the related defenses are working well, then the phobic object recedes and a general state of anxiety—itself varying in degree—arises. In precarious conditions however when these defenses are weakened, or when a series of discomforting signifiers come to light, then a more overtly fearful condition comes to the fore.

The atmosphere of a vague and undefined dread that the story sketches is the result of at least two operations of the unconscious. It has, for a start, been partially separated off from its most direct phobic object, that of the dangerous and violent black man. This is of course one variant on Fanon's phobogenic object in *Black Skin White Mask* (1986): the violent Black criminal. Signifier and affect have thus been—however provisionally—detached. The psychical operation of displacement is in effect here; in a way similar to obsessional rituals, a series of anxious activities (locking up the outside room, securing the household tools) has taken the place of a dreadful thought that cannot be confronted directly. Secondly, the affect itself, a composite of fear and guilt, has been attenuated, such that it is not directly experienced as such, but occurs rather as a cloud of unease, a sense that something—something difficult to pinpoint—is not right. Such a redistribution of affect brings with it pros and cons for the person experiencing it: the severity of phobic experience is diluted, yet virtually anything, any object, can take on a fearful aspect as a result. (We might note, incidentally, that the feeling conveyed by the story, the sense of stagnancy, of social and subjective malaise, is not dissimilar to Crapanzano's (1985) description of the inhibition of creativity, enjoyment and social intercourse brought about by oppressive states of waiting).

I noted earlier, following Crapanzano's (1985) paraphrasing of Freud, that the attempt to reduce anxiety often results in sacrificing 'reality' to 'psychic need'. This seems precisely the relation on display in the extract, where a fearful eventuality is, as it were, 'actively' constructed, 'willingly' made, even if in a largely unconscious capacity. This perhaps helps to explain why such dreadful scenes of vengeful and racialized violence are believed in, why racist caricatures of black criminals are constantly (if, for the most part *tacitly*) affirmed and reiterated in the white post-apartheid imaginary. Such stereotypical figures are believed in, because—as is the case with all fantasy—they are 'more real than real', and because a clearly-delineated phobic object is invariably preferable to an object-less state of anxiety.

There is a further conceptual gain in qualifying the fear as unconscious, subject to repression. Here it pays to underline that the story, and the fantasmatic scenario it includes, is of childhood. Likewise worth noting is the fact that not all of what is remembered within the context of the narrative is overtly anxious or fearful. Take for instance the last lines of the story, in which the character of the boy dwells of the memory of an ornamental wooden box (a smaller version of the trunks? another repository of family secrets?) in his parents' bedroom:

> This box, with its unpolished brass hinges, its unfinished, grainy interior, will stay with him forever. Whatever location it may be moved to, it will always pull him back to the open window in his parents' bedroom that overlooks the back garden where the dogs play, where the leaking tap feeds the sprinkler, on a Saturday afternoon.

It is not only the temporality of dread that is contained within the story. The narrative speaks also of the endless persistence of memory that lives on, as sharp and bright as the moment it was experienced. This unconscious preservation of childhood and early family experience underlines for us the potential indestructibility of the fear—and the guilt—in question. It stresses, moreover, the *inter-generational* quality of what is being conveyed. (What is indestructible can here be read as that which is continually past on, never fully processed or 'worked through'). To bypass this facet of the repressed is to miss out on a fertile avenue of analysis, one that is both empirically-rich and more historically-grounded than the murky postulate of 'primordial fear'. The concept of trans-generational guilt would, incidentally, provide a novel perspective on the narrative discussed above, drawing attention to those facets of the child's environment and future life haunted by a political past that has been inadequately symbolized, or 'de-repressed'.[11] What such a possible research agenda alerts us to is the possibility that the guilt (unconscious or otherwise) and the white anxiety to which it is invariably linked, may be ripening, and may yet be more vividly expressed (or repressed) by a subsequent generation of white South Africans.

Contrary to Mbembe's general theoretical speculations on the sociality of temporality, this account in anchored in the texture of a singular subjectivity. While this might sometimes be considered a problem—a reduction of the complexity of the social to the parameters of the merely subjective—it may also represent a genuine analytical opportunity, certainly so if we allow that the domain of individual experience can, under certain circumstances, reflect with heightened clarity aspects of broader repressed social experience. If one is take seriously the hope of the *de-subjectivization* of social structure, the aim, that is to say, of over-turning constrictive or inhibiting forms of temporality, then we surely we cannot forego that which psychoanalysis has always prioritized: the sustained engagement with the particularities of individual subjectivities.

The Time of Malaise

Does the above narrative contain a moral, perhaps about how racism engenders its own fearful sense of future recriminations? The disturbance of temporality in question here is, in many respects, the result of racist social structure, and more specifically, of an instance of racist violence—real or imagined—that has produced its own fearful and subjective sense of the inevitability of recrimination. Importantly—and this is crucial to appreciating the psychoanalytic contribution to (post)apartheid temporalities—the temporality in question is mediated by fantasy, by the realm of unconscious belief. Of course, the idea that racism generates its own anxieties in an endlessly self-perpetuating way is not a new thesis; this idea is found in several of Homi Bhabha's (1994) early essays. Nonetheless, stressing how this facet of racism results in a particular experience of time—the temporality of retribution—does offer something of a contribution to thinking the temporality of the post-apartheid. The story evokes this dimension of temporality subtly, but effectively; it arouses a sense of the stagnancy and heaviness of time that refuses to pass, a congealed time, whose intimations of recrimination are permanent, ineradicable.[12]

What cultural tropes might help us further articulate the state of fearful expectancy invoked in the above narrative? As already noted, what is in question is not merely waiting, but a time of *suspended judgement*. A host of mythical and/or religious themes converge here: the concepts of purgatory and limbo, the notion of a Day of Reckoning, and the idea shared by Judaism and Christianity alike, of ancestral sin—particularly apt given the above narrative—namely, that the "sins of the father" (or of one generation) might be passed down. This alerts us to a further consideration not explored by Crapanzano (1985). It is not just a sense of the inevitability of change that underscores the anxiety of white waiting during (and after) apartheid, but all the mythical (which is also to say fantasmatic) resonances set in play by the ideas of fate, by the presumption that there might be a balancing of the scales of justice.

It is often remarked that South Africa's transition was secured without a bloodbath or a civil war. This observation is sometimes accompanied by the remark that apartheid's white beneficiaries were never made to pay, that they were not held accountable for the past. True as this may be, the suspension of punishment, much like the proverbial Sword of Damocles, often brings its own psychical cost. John Pilger's famous (1996) political pronouncement that 'apartheid did not die' is given a new inflection here: the guilt for apartheid has not died either. There are presumably those within the broad mass of white beneficiaries of various global/historical instantiations of racism who feel some degree of culpability for it, and who believe, despite conscious attitudes to the contrary, that they deserve punishment. There are also, surely, some who maintain the unconscious conviction that such punishment will, at some indeterminate point, arrive. It once again helps to cite Fanon here, especially in respect of his reflections on the traumatic inheritance of colonialism: "The disaster of the man of color lies in the fact that he has was enslaved. The disaster [or calamity] and inhumanity of the white man lies in the fact that somewhere he has killed man" (1952/231, p. 231). The various lingering sequalae of this (repressed) site of guilt is one source of—one fantasmatic element of—what Robin DiAngelo (2011) has referred to as white fragility. We have here thus one variant of the temporality of white anxiety.

There is something of the terrorizing logic of the superego to this experience of delayed retribution. Anxiety is presumably increased the more a deserved punishment does not come. By being forever delayed, the threat is amplified; because the penalty cannot be paid, the scales of justice cannot be balanced. Perhaps the best psychoanalytic description of the temporality described in the above narrative would simply be—the time of the superego.[13] In a brief discussion of 'Some character types met with in psychoanalytic work', Freud (1916) speaks of subjects who suffer from oppressive feelings of guilt and who appear to seek out forms of punishment that will allow them a sense of relief from such a free-floating sense of guiltiness. In *Civilization and its Discontents* (1930) Freud remarks: “there are types of patients who are not aware of their sense of guilt, or who only feel it as a tormenting uneasiness, a kind of anxiety” (p. 135). The punishments that the subject subsequently unconsciously gravitates toward may take on a variety of different forms, from accidental acts perpetrated against the self, to putting oneself in dangerous situations and assorted irrationally reckless behaviors. Interestingly, for Freud (1930), there are many such subjects who remain unaware of their sense of guilt, “who only feel it as a tormenting uneasiness, a kind of anxiety ... a sort of *malaise*” (p. 135).[14]

In closing this section let me cite a literary example that provides an eloquent expression of the unconscious dynamics of retribution (the wish for, or relief in, punishment) in the post-apartheid context. I have in mind the figure of Lucy in J.M. Coetzee’s *Disgrace*, who resignedly accepts the violent attack and rape she is subjected to by the Black men who had previously worked as laborers for her. The fact that she wishes no form of retribution on her assailants is incomprehensible to her father, David, who was horribly wounded in the attack. The difference of response of these two characters can be read as indicative of two ‘guilt-positions’, two subjective orientations—indeed, two modes of temporal experience—relative to the white anxieties of retribution brought about the end of apartheid. Even though Lucy has endured a horrific ordeal, the psychoanalytic point could be made that this event entails a paradoxically consoling quality, inasmuch as it implies a balancing of the scales, the enactment of a brutal punishment that will alleviate the anxiety of further retribution and guilt.[15]

Conclusion

I have argued elsewhere (Hook, 2013) that the temporality of South Africa’s (post)apartheid period of political transition is unique, a time in which accelerations and apparent ‘slow-downs’ and reversals of history coexist alongside anxious periods of stasis, suspension and retroaction. Apt a characterization as this may be, it is hard, particularly given the preceding discussion, to avoid a predominant motif in the analysis of (post)apartheid temporality, namely that of a type of arrested time—or petrified life—whether this be understood along the lines of repetition, nostalgia fixity, the suspension of anxious/fearful waiting, or the time of guilt.

What then have we learnt as a result of the juxtaposition of the foregoing contributions to the conceptualization of (post)apartheid temporality? Well, we have, as a result of adopting a psychoanalytic perspective, been able to foreground a series of missed analytical opportunities in the literature. This is true both at the level of particular concepts (repetition compulsion, screen memories, libidinal attachment, deferred action, repression) and in terms of a series of associated areas of analysis that a psychoanalytic perspective would accordingly prioritize (the material of individual subjectivity, the domain of fantasy, the dynamic operation of the unconscious, and, potentially, the dimension of inter-generational affects).

In addition to this, we have been confronted with the somewhat jarring realization that the contemporary post-apartheid exhibits a series of striking similarities to the temporality of the late apartheid era. Crapanzano's (1985) concepts of deadened time and de-realized experience correspond with Mbembe's (2008, 2013) ideas of the deathliness of repetition and the virtuality of nostalgic fixity, a fact which allows us to consider the disturbing prospect, noted above, that the post-apartheid present is the deferred action of apartheid itself. This suggests that the temporality of suspension that characterized the closing months of apartheid is not unique. (One thinks of Gordimer's (1983) Gramscian declaration that in South Africa the "historical coordinates don't fit life any longer" (p. 22), her insistence that the late apartheid era was tantamount to a period of interregnum.) Nor is it separated by a radical discontinuity from select aspects of post-apartheid experience. Indeed, the 'futurity' of Crapanzano's account, and the anxious interchange of an unstable present and an unknown future, could be said to pertain just as much to the post-apartheid as the apartheid context.

I made brief mention above of Browne's (2014) notion of polytemporality, that is, the idea of a complex of varied intersecting modalities of temporality that result in the production of distinctive experiences and discursive formations. As fascinating as the literature on adjacent or combined temporalities is (Bastian, 2011; Chakrabarty, 2000; Fabian, 1983), it often leaves unspecified the specificity of the relation between the temporal modes in question. This leads to the third speculative conclusion of this chapter. Might it be the case that the varied forms of arrested temporality discussed above (repetition, nostalgic fixity, the deadened experience of anxious/fearful waiting, the unending time of retribution) come to work in tandem, in a relation of combination and mutual reiteration? The benefit of the conceptualization of petrified life is apparent here: these ostensibly separate and distinct modes of temporality can be read as interlocking forms, as linked temporal modes, each of which plays its part in engendering a type of historical immobilization characterized by states of suspension, stasis and fear. This would suggest that the historical categories of oppressor and oppressed—apartheid's beneficiaries and victims alike—each (perhaps unintentionally, unconsciously) potentially play their part in the temporal resistance to structural change. While we do not have enough evidence to convincingly mount such a claim here—the focus of the current discussion is, admittedly, predominantly on white experiences of temporality—we may allow it stand in the form of a hypothesis: are there varying forms of arrested time, of petrified life, that unite what may otherwise be understood as distinct or even oppositional social or political groupings?

Before closing, it is worthwhile pointing to an apparent limitation of the above approach. Despite the benefits of analytical appraisals of how modalities of time become operative in relation to specific historical situations ("apartheid", the "post-colonial" etc.), do such attempts not implicitly lend themselves to normative understandings of how time properly or realistically unfolds? The implicit presumption is that outside the range of various political forms of disturbance, temporality would be somehow neutral, evenly paced, lacking in defensive distortions. Perhaps the only satisfying response to this challenge is simply to note that psychical time—presumably much like psychical experience itself—is never merely neutral. Temporality thus understood cannot exist in a state evacuated of fantasmatic contents; it is always an exception to what might be considered purely symbolic time. What psychoanalysis maintains of fantasy—that is, the necessarily perspectival framework through which we have access to experience—seems true also of temporality. Should we succeed in removing all the distortions and idiosyncrasies concerning how reality is effectively framed, we would not have a pristine objective reality (or temporality), but no access to reality (or temporality) at all. Differently put, temporality exists only in distorted forms (as 'time-out-of-joint'), there is no normative model.[16]

There are of course those would contest the suggestions offered above, namely that late apartheid and contemporary post-apartheid temporalities are under-differentiated, that the post-apartheid era is a period in which the (genuinely) new is still struggling to be born. To this we might point to an apparent failure of the post-apartheid social imaginary, and ask: what is it that comes *after* the post-apartheid, and why does it seem so extraordinarily difficult to provide a convincing answer to this question?

Notes

1. I am indebted to Victoria Browne's (2014) argument that historical time should be approached and theorized as a form of *lived time* in order to guard "against the reduction of historical time to the realm of pure textuality" and so as to oppose "scientific and metaphysical approaches that are interested in time as an objective condition or phenomenon" (p. 26).
2. I mark here some distance to Browne's (2014) notion of lived time. Whereas she expresses reservations about the reduction of historical time to "the realm of … the imagination" (p. 26), my psychoanalytic interests clearly lie with considering precisely the fantasmatic dimension of time.
3. I should qualify the use of 'ethical' here. The term is meant in the clinical psychoanalytic sense, i.e. as pertaining to what assists change in the subject.
4. Much the same argument is made by the literary scholar David Medalie (2010) in respect of instances of nostalgia in post-apartheid literature. In opposition to intricate forms nostalgia that open up the possibility of reinvention and the fashioning of the new, he notes a type of unreflecting nostalgia that fails to subject the past to adequate interrogation. He interestingly notes, furthermore, how given formal features—stereotypical, unimaginative narrative components, flatness of characters, evident artifice,—might be read precisely as an index of the failure of more creative and critical uses of the nostalgic impulse.
5. Lacan puts it this way: "something … freezes the flow of memory … reduces it … by arresting it at this point called a screen-memory. Think of how cinematographic motion can be speeding along altogether rapidly and then all of a sudden stop at some point, capturing the characters in a freeze-frame … [We have thus] the reduction of the full signifying scene … to something immobilized in … fantasy, which remains charged with … the erotic values … of which it remains the testimony and the support, the last support that remains" (2020, p. 112).
6. If we were to identify a 'vanishing mediator' linking the concept of petrification in Mbembe (who, to stress once again, does not explicitly utilize the term) and Crapanzano it would have to be Fanon. In *The Wretched of the Earth*, Fanon (1965) speaks of the world of settler-colonialism as a "motionless, petrified world" (p. 78), noting, later in the text, that "The appearance of the settler has meant… the death of the aboriginal society, cultural lethargy, and the petrification of individuals" (p. 93).
7. This, the question of how variant temporalities relate to one another within an over-arching shared temporal mode, represents a point of considerable debate in the literature on political temporality (Bastian, 2011; Chakrabarty, 2000; Fabian, 1983). I have found Browne's (2014) notion of 'complex coevalness' suggestive in this respect. This is the idea—clearly pertinent to

the post-apartheid context—that we exist in a state of temporal entanglement, a condition in which "different historical temporalities…may interrelate and intersect … [without being] "additive" parts of a greater totality or whole" (Browne, 2014, pp. 41–2). Such a sharing of time, does not, however presume an ironing out of temporal differences, or an expunging of political differences (Browne, 2014).

8. An interesting example of this is to be found in Steve Biko's defiant assertion, offered as part of a defense of Black Consciousness comrades accused of treasonous activities in an apartheid court of law:

   > [W]e, as blacks, must articulate what we want, and put it across to the white man… We have analysed history. We believe that history moves in a particular logical direction, and in this instance, the logical direction is that eventually any white society in this country is going to have to accommodate black thinking. We are mere agents in that history. (Biko, cited in Woods, 1978, p. 185)

   Although these words are spoken several years before Crapanzano's study commenced, they provide supportive evidence of sorts not only for his emphasis on a temporal imaginary in apartheid, but for his suggestion that waiting assumes the quality of hope for those most oppressed under apartheid.
9. We might refer here, again, to Biko (1978) as a means of corroborating Crapanzano's assertion. In 'Fear – an important determinant in South African politics', a chapter within his *I Write What I Like* (1978), Biko speaks of how the fear of white brutality "erodes the soul of black people in South Africa", of the racist "*swart gevaar*" (or "black peril") nurtured by whites, and, furthermore of how "this interaction between fear and reaction sets on a vicious cycle that … makes meaningful coalitions between black and white totally impossible" (1978, p. 77).
10. If we were to adhere more strictly to the technical vocabulary of psychoanalysis we would need to stress how the fear has in effect been *displaced*, which is to say that it has been (at least partially) disconnected from a given idea, differently distributed, and, in this case, attenuated. Strictly speaking, and as Freud (1924) affirms, affects cannot be 'repressed' (made wholly unconscious) although repressive measures—precisely such as that of displacement—play their part in relocating the affects in question, in de-attachment them to certain signifiers and re-attaching them to others. I retain the use of 'repressed' and 'repression' here in a general descriptive sense and so as to invoke the dynamism of the psychical mechanisms in question.

11. The idea of trans-generational guilt represents an important area of psychoanalytic enquiry—see Fogelman, 1988, Rothe (2012), Stierlin (1974) and Wiseman et al. (2006)—which, unfortunately, I cannot pursue further here. Suffice for the time being to say that the concept provides a promising means of extending the current study of post-apartheid temporality.
12. This, of course, is a hallmark of Freud's (1933) notion of the unconscious, that its contents are indestructible, 'immortal'.
13. To say that whites were not made to pay for apartheid is not of course to say that this idea was never muted in some or other form, or indeed, that such a possibility has not featured as a possibility within the minds of many white South Africans. Quite the contrary—the idea, even in its more subtle forms, proves to be a reoccurring motif in South African public culture. One might cite here Desmond Tutu's muted "wealth tax" to be imposed on whites; the performative role of a figure like Julius Malema (the leader of the political party, EFF (Economic Freedom Fighters)) as a type of white folk-devil (Falkof, 2014); or political promises, advanced by the EFF to redistribute the country's wealth, to expropriate land without compensation, and to nationalize mines and banks, etc. Such an unconscious fear of retribution would provide a perspective also, perhaps obviously, on the ever-present phenomenon of white crime fear.
14. The link that I have treated somewhat tenuously, and subjected to a psychoanalytic reading—that between crime-fear and punishment—is given a far more direct expression by Joelien Pretorius (2014), who comments that white crime fear in South Africa has been produced in discourse precisely "as a way for blacks to make whites pay for apartheid", after all, this was something blacks "were denied the chance to do by the formal negotiation and the Truth and Reconciliation Process" (2014, p. 29). This factor of discomfort at not being punished, is given eloquent expression by Antjie Krog, a journalist and poet who offered one of the most heartfelt and searching engagements with South Africa's Truth and Reconciliation Commission:

    > White people were prepared for the worst at the hands of a black government. What they weren't prepared for was to be forgiven. It made and still makes whites deeply uncomfortable…[for] we understand hatred…we admire revenge. (2009, p. 206)

15. The same of course cannot be said for Lucy's father, whose recalcitrance in respect of his own guilt—arguably the principle theme of the novel—remains unresolved.

16. The methodology of the psychoanalytic clinic proves instructive here: to note distortions—highly differentiated forms of temporality, say—does not necessarily tie one to an ideal reference-point. The epistemology of psychoanalysis is distinctive in this respect: clinicians aim at grappling with the particularities of psychical reality (fantasy) without constant reference either to the bench-mark of actual 'objective' reality or to those of normative social ideals.

References

Abbas, A. (2011). Thinking through images: Turkishness and its discontents: A Commentary. *New Perspectives on Turkey, 45*, 215–226.

Anderson, B. (2009). Affective atmospheres. *Emotion, Space & Society, 2*, 77–81.

Apartheid Archive Project. (2010). Apartheid Archive Project. Retrieved from https://www.communityidentity.com.au/portfolio/the-apartheid-archives-project/

Barnard, R. (2014). Introduction. In R. Barnard (Ed.), *The Cambridge Companion to Nelson Mandela*. Cambridge University of Cambridge Press.

Bastian, M. (2011). The contradictory simultaneity of being with others: Exploring concepts of time and community in the work of Gloria Anzaldua. *Feminist Review, 97*, 151–167.

Bhabha, H. K. (1994). *The Location of Culture*. Routledge.

Biko, S. (1978). *I Write What I Like*. Bowerdean.

Bowman, B., Duncan, N., & Sonn, C. (2010). Towards a psychology of South Africa's histories: Living with and through the Apartheid Archive. *South Africa Journal of Psychology, 40*(4), 365–369.

Browne, V. (2014). *Feminism, Time, and Nonlinear History*. Palgrave.

Chakrabarty, D. (2000). *Provincializing Europe: Postcolonial Thought and Historical Difference*. Princeton University Press.

Crapanzano, V. (1985). *Waiting: The Whites of South Africa*. Granada.

DiAngelo, R. (2011). White fragility. *International Journal of Critical Pedagogy, 3*(3), 54–70.

Duncan, N., Stevens, G., & Sonn, C. S. (2012). Of narratives and nostalgia. *Peace and Conflict: Journal of Peace Psychology, 18*(3), 205–213.

Eagle, G., & Bowman, B. (2010). Thinking about self-representation in the narrative-based Apartheid Archive Project. *Psychology in Society, 40*, 29–48.

Fabian, J. (1983). *Time and the Other: How Anthropology Makes its Object*. Columbia University Press.

Falkof, N. (2014). Talking the (white) talk; walking the (white) walk. *Daily Maverick*, 19 June.

Fanon, F. (1965). *The Wretched of the Earth*. Grove Press.

Fanon, F. (1986). *Black Skin, White Masks*. Pluto.

Fogelman, E. (1988). Intergenerational group therapy: Child survivors of the holocaust and offspring of survivors. *Psychoanalytic Review, 75*(4), 619–640.

Forde, F. (2011). *An Inconvenient Youth – Julius Malema and the New ANC*. Picador Africa.

Freud, S. (1893). Sexuality in the Aetiology of the Neuroses. In S. Freud (1966–1974), *The Standard Edition of the Complete Psychological Works of Sigmund Freud* (Vol. III, J. Strachey, Trans.). Vintage, Hogarth Press and Institute of Psycho-Analysis.

Freud, S. (1899). Screen Memories. In S. Freud (1966–1974), *The Standard Edition of the Complete Psychological Works of Sigmund Freud* (Vol. III, J. Strachey, Trans.). Vintage, Hogarth Press and Institute of Psycho-Analysis.

Freud, S. (1916). Some Character Types met with in Psychoanalytic Work. In S. Freud (1966–1974), *The Standard Edition of the Complete Psychological Works of Sigmund Freud* (Vol. XIV, J. Strachey, Trans.). Vintage, Hogarth Press and Institute of Psycho-Analysis.

Freud, S. (1920). Beyond the Pleasure Principle. In S. Freud (1966–1974), *The Standard Edition of the Complete Psychological Works of Sigmund Freud* (Vol. XIIX, J. Strachey, Trans.). Vintage, Hogarth Press and Institute of Psycho-Analysis.

Freud, S. (1924). The Economic Problem of Masochism. In S. Freud (1966–1974), *The Standard Edition of the Complete Psychological Works of Sigmund Freud* (Vol. XIX, J. Strachey, Trans.). Vintage, Hogarth Press and Institute of Psycho-Analysis.

Freud, S. (1926). Inhibitions, Symptoms and Anxiety. In S. Freud (1966–1974), *The Standard Edition of the Complete Psychological Works of Sigmund Freud* (Vol. XX, J. Strachey, Trans.). Vintage, Hogarth Press and Institute of Psycho-Analysis.

Freud, S. (1930). Civilization and its Discontents. In S. Freud (1966–1974), *The Standard Edition of the Complete Psychological Works of Sigmund Freud* (Vol. XXI, J. Strachey, Trans.). Vintage, Hogarth Press and Institute of Psycho-Analysis

Freud, S. (1933). New Introductory Lectures. In S. Freud (1966–1974), *The Standard Edition of the Complete Psychological Works of Sigmund Freud* (Vol. XXII, J. Strachey, Trans.). Vintage, Hogarth Press and Institute of Psycho-Analysis.

Freud, S. (1950). Project for a Scientific Psychology. In S. Freud (1966–1974), *The Standard Edition of the Complete Psychological Works of Sigmund Freud* (Vol. I, J. Strachey, Trans.). Vintage, Hogarth Press and Institute of Psycho-Analysis.

Frosh, S. (2011). *Psychoanalysis Outside the Clinic: Interventions in Psychosocial Studies*. Palgrave.

Gordimer, N. (1983). Living in the interregnum. *New York Review of Books, XXIX*, 21–29.

Hook, D. (2013). *(Post)apartheid Conditions: Psychoanalysis and Social Formation*. Palgrave.
Hook, D., & Long, C. (2011). The Apartheid Archive Project, heterogeneity, and the psychoanalysis of racism. *Psychoanalysis, Culture & Society, 16*, 1–10.
Krog, A. (2009). *Begging to be Black*. Random House.
Lacan, J. (2020). In Jacques-Alain Miller (Ed.), *The Seminar of Jacques Lacan, Book IV: The Object Relation* (A. Price, Trans.). Polity Press.
Mbembe, A. (2008). Aesthetics of Superfluity. In S. Nuttall & A. Mbembe (Eds.), *Johannesburg the Elusive Metropolis*. Wits University Press.
Mbembe, A. (2013). Consumed by our lust for lost segregation. *Mail & Guardian*, 29 March to 4 April, p. 29.
Medalie, D. (2010). The uses of nostalgia. *English Studies in Africa, 53*(1), 35–44.
Osbourne, P. (1995). *The Politics of Time: Modernity and Avant-garde*. Verso.
Pilger, J. (1996). *Freedom Next Time*. Black Swan.
Pretorius, J. (2014). "Dubul' Ibhunu" (Shoot the boer): A psycho-political analysis of farm attacks in South Africa. *Psychology in Society, 47*, 21–40.
Rothe, K. (2012). Anti-Semitism in Germany today and the intergenerational transmission of guilt and shame. *Psychoanalysis, Culture & Society, 17*, 16–34.
Saville-Young, L. (2011). Research entanglements, race and recognisability: A psychosocial reading of interview encounters in (post-)colonial, (post-)apartheid South Africa. *Qualitative Inquiry, 17*(1), 45–55.
Stevens, G., & Laubscher, L. (2010). Editorial: Facing the apartheid archive. *Psychology in Society, 40*, 1–7.
Stevens, G., Duncan, N., & Hook, D. (2013). *Race, Memory and the Apartheid Archive*. Palgrave.
Stierlin, H. (1974). Shame and guilt in family relations—Theoretical and clinical aspects. *Archives of General Psychiatry, 30*(3), 381–389.
Wiseman, H., Metzl, E., & Barber, J. P. (2006). Anger, guilt, and intergenerational communication of trauma in the interpersonal narratives of second generation holocaust survivors. *American Journal of Orthopsychiatry, 76*(2), 176–184.
Woods, D. (1978). *Biko*. Penguin.

CHAPTER 3

White Anxiety

Abstract Robin DiAngelo's (*White Fragility*, Beacon Press, 2018) influential notion of white fragility while certainly suggestive and critically useful, does not go quite far enough in accounting for aspects of white anxiety as it manifests in the post-apartheid context. The first step in my reconsideration of this concept is to present a series of distinctive examples of white anxiety in the (post)apartheid context. I make reference to literary accounts, interview data, and to what is perhaps the crowning accomplishment of dystopian South African science-fiction, Neil Blomkamp's 2009 film *District 9.* I then turn to Lacanian psychoanalysis to sketch a rudimentary paradigm of anxiety, one which highlights a variety of interlocking levels of anxiety: (1) 'realistic' anxiety at the prospect of death, (2) imaginary anxiety related to a failing self-image, (3) anxiety pertaining to symbolic inter-subjectivity and the desires of an Other, and (4) anxiety as the incapacitation of desire. A perhaps unexpected implication of the reading that I offer is that beneath the racist defensiveness of much post-apartheid whiteness we can often detect an ambiguous mode of unconscious identification with otherness, an identification with the prospect of being something other than what one is.

Keywords Fantasy • Psychoanalysis • South Africa • Science fiction • Suicide • 'White fragility' • Whiteness

D. Hook, *Whiteness at the Abyss*, The Palgrave Lacan Series,
https://doi.org/10.1007/978-3-031-78509-2_3

Although the post-apartheid era of South African history formally began 30 years ago, when Nelson Mandela's African National Congress won the country's first free democratic elections (in April 1994), the legacy of white supremacy remains forcibly in place. Hegemonic formations of whiteness—in the forms of white privilege, white ownership of the means of production, disproportionate white wealth—still very clearly exist, and whiteness retains formidable cultural power as a marker of normative values and ideals.[1] Much of South Africa remains, as Tendayi Sithole has recently (2024) argued, a territory of unfreedom for Blacks. Nonetheless, the distinctive socio-historical formation of South African whiteness stands apart from that of many other settler or formerly colonial nations (the United States, Australia, Canada, etc.) in which whites still constitute a democratic and cultural majority (Steyn, 1998, 2004). This is decidedly not the case in South Africa, where whites make up around 7.3% of the population compared to 81.4% of Black Africans. Arguably then, South African instantiations of whiteness, as opposed to those of many other settler societies, have been forced to take on altered or re-negotiated forms for the simple reason that whites are now a clear and shrinking minority in the country.

Direct and often highly critical challenges to whiteness are now a common and indeed unavoidable part of everyday, mainstream political discourse in South Africa. A clear research imperative then lies with conceptualizing the affective, psychical, and psychosocial states that characterize South African whiteness at its most fragile, anxious, and threatened. We might ask: does South Africa represent something of a test case in respect of the future of whiteness in other global contexts? Or, more particularly: do we find in South Africa a comparative context for other domains in which whiteness is needs to forego its previously naturalized assumptions of cultural and political dominance?

A brief example suffices to illustrate something of the state of whiteness under threat in post-apartheid South Africa. In early 2016, a young white academic and colleague, Terblanche Delport, sparked outrage at a Johannesburg conference at the University of the Witwatersrand. As part of the imagined demise of structures of white privilege, Delport called on white people in South Africa "to commit suicide as an ethical act". Or, as was reported by the PRAAG (Pro-Afrikaans Action Group) website: 'A lecturer in philosophy yesterday said at a radical anti-white, anti-Afrikaner conference at the University of the Witwatersrand that "whites should die".' Here is perhaps the most controversial part of his written paper:

> The reality [in South Africa] is that most white people spend their whole lives only engaging [B]lack people in subservient positions – cleaners, gardeners, etc. My question is then how can a person not be racist if that's the way they live their lives? The only way then for white people to become part of Africa is to not exist as white people anymore. If the goal is to dismantle white supremacy, and white supremacy is white culture and vice versa, then the goal has to be to dismantle white culture and ultimately white people themselves. The total integration into Africa by white people will also automatically then mean the death of white people as white as a concept would not exist anymore. (Delport, 2016, p. 1)

Controversial as Delport's statements were, it seems clear upon reading the above extract—the provocative mention of "the death of white people" notwithstanding—that his primary target was white privilege, that is, white culture within South Africa as structure of domination (Ahmed, 2007; Ngo, 2017; Yancy, 2012). Delport was, of course, not alone in offering such a speculative picturing of white demise, as the titles of two books published at around the same time makes clear—Ferial Haffajee's (2015) *What if there were no Whites in South Africa?* and Nicky Falkof's (2016) *The End of Whiteness.*

Calls for a type of 'death of whiteness' offered as a political prerequisite for meaningful anti-racist structural change, as an ethical task, paradoxically enough, for whiteness itself, have also been offered in other contexts. Consider for example George Yancy's comments in his (2018) book *Backlash*:

> [T]here are certain forms of death that are necessary. The oppressive machinations of whiteness must die so that white people (*you*) can truly live. What is meant by this death? It involves an opening, a risk, a fissure. As white, you must be open to a kind of death, a death of your stubbornness, a death of your denials, a death of your "innocence," a death of your arrogance, a death of your racial comfort, a death of your narcissism, a death of your "goodness," a death of your fears, a death of your color evasion, a death of your self-righteousness, a death of your sense of entitlement, a death of your illusions of safety, a death of your sense of "greatness" and "manifest destiny," a death of all of those tricks that you play to convince yourselves that you are fine, that you are the good ones, the sophisticated ones, the nonracist ones, the ones who truly care about justice and a world without oppression, hatred, and racist violence. (Yancy, 2018, p. 58)

Although commentary of this sort is often read as nothing more than aggression against whites, as a wish to do away with white people, let me stress, at the risk of redundancy, that Yancy's comments can or should be read as an ethical invitation to take up transformative anti-racist practices and ways of being in the world.[2] In this respect they make for an effective counterpart to Delport's remarks.

Predictably enough, Delport's comments occasioned uproar.[3] There seemed to be a degree of willful misunderstanding at work in such retorts. Delport emphasized that his was a provocation, a rhetorical act, an ethical gesture rather than—as one would imagine was quite obvious—a literal suggestion. Ultimately one might say that Delport's point was made more in *the responses* to his provocation than in the provocation itself. This is where I want to pick up the thread: by arguing that there was something potentially ethical in Delport's statements. Delport took his white audience to a space of contemplated racial demise, to the threshold of a type of symbolic extinction, to a proposed 'end of whiteness'. It is precisely this site of anxiety that concerns us here. Such examples of white anxiety are omnipresent in both the post-apartheid context and elsewhere, and they are to be found in both dramatic and mundane instances, as underling both intellectual discourse and everyday dilemmas of identity.

White Fragility in the Elusive Metropolis

In 2011, Robin DiAngelo coined the concept of 'white fragility' which she defined as:

> [A] state in which even a minimum of racial stress becomes intolerable, triggering a range of defensive moves. These moves include the outward display of emotions such as anger, fear, and guilt, and behaviours such as argumentation, silence, and leaving the stress-inducing situation. These behaviours, in turn, function to reinstate white racial equilibrium. (2011, p. 54)

In offering this definition, DiAngelo is indebted to series of influential theorists of whiteness (Fine, 1997; Frankenberg, 1993; Dyer, 1997; Ngo, 2017), who, DiAngelo tells us, have used the notion to signify a set of locations that are historically, socially, politically and culturally constructed and that are intrinsically linked to dynamic relations of domination. Whiteness is thus "a constellation of processes and practices rather than a discrete entity" (DiAngelo, 2011, p. 56).

Like several recent theorists of whiteness (Bonilla-Silva, 2017; Bonilla-Silva et al., 2006; Ngo, 2017), DiAngelo draws inspiration from Bourdieu's (1993) influential notion of the habitus, which helps us understand how whiteness

> produces and reproduces thoughts, perceptions, expressions and actions. Strategies of response to "disequilibrium" in the habitus are not based on conscious intentionality but rather result from unconscious dispositions towards practice and depend on the power position the agent occupies in the social structure. (DiAngelo, 2011, p. 58)

In *White Fragility*, DiAngelo (2018) develops and clarifies her position, noting that this titular concept is "much more than mere defensiveness or whining. It may be conceptualized as the sociology of dominance: an outcome of white people's socialization into white supremacy and a means to protect, maintain, and reproduce white supremacy" (2018, p. 113). This is a crucial qualification, one which reminds us that DiAngelo's concerns are primarily sociological and political; she is primarily focused on whiteness as a historical structure of oppression. Nevertheless, in responding to DiAngelo's work from a psychoanalytic perspective, I am drawn to the aspect of white defensiveness that she so aptly describes when warning that "pointing out white advantage will often trigger patterns of confusion, defensiveness, and righteous indignation" (2018, p. 109). Part, then, of what most appeals to me about the idea of white fragility is that it highlights a mode of experience that comes to the fore in moments when white subjects feel themselves to be out of place. Without wanting to reduce DiAngelo's conceptualization to one aspect of her broader account, and freely admitting that I am attempting, psychoanalytically, to develop a particular facet of this account, I want to argue that the notion of white fragility can be read as a theory of dislocation. Doing so highlights a series of critical prospects that may otherwise have remained latent within her conceptualization.

Thinking the idea of white fragility as a theory of dislocation has the advantage, firstly, of highlighting that white fragility has a crucial *positional* dimension. There is, in DiAngelo's (2011) account, a recurring emphasis on whiteness as situated, as a *located* and thereby also symbolic and historically grounded set of habits, responses and dispositions. Secondly, an emphasis on the aspect of dislocation brings to the fore a dimension that DiAngelo does not adequately discuss, but that is nonetheless crucial—certainly with the South African context—namely a sense of whiteness as vulnerable, as something that can be fragmented, broken, even destroyed. It stresses, in other words, how whiteness is itself a kind of nervous condition (see also Falkof, 2014; Steyn, 2004). We might make reference to a more historical account here in referring to the work of Melissa Steyn (1998), who effectively foregrounds the tremulous conditions of white colonial subjectivity in the Southern African context:

> The Africans, among whom these "whites" had come to settle, had a legitimacy on the continent (determinedly undermined by the successive "white" regimes) and a sense of connection with their ancient cultures (damaged, but never destroyed by colonial conquest and apartheid). And given the numerical superiority of Africans, their reserves could always be replenished, despite repeated defeats [...] Deep-seated feelings of alienation, personal threat and fear of being overrun were held in tension with an intense competition for resources and an absolute belief in entitlement to dominate people with whom one had daily contact in one's home. (p. 268)

Thirdly, the factor of dislocation, of literally being out of place, clearly also possesses a concrete spatial and geographical dimension. It is no coincidence, in this respect, that virtually all the examples I draw on in this chapter stem from Johannesburg. Johannesburg is not only the most densely populated, racially diverse and rapidly changing city in South Africa—bearing out Achille Mbembe and Sarah Nuttall's (2008) description of the city as both 'the elusive metropolis' and a globalized African mega-city (indeed, an 'Afropolis')—it is also the country's cultural and economic hub, characterized by a high rate of daily border crossings between different and often geographically proximate yet sharply divergent socio-economic and racial zones.[4] Of all South African cities—and the influx of Africa immigration into the city over the last decade plays a key role here—Johannesburg retains the greatest prospect of destabilizing 'racial encounters' (Durrheim & Dixon, 2014), the greatest possibility of whiteness being dislocated, experiencing itself as visible, vulnerable and thereby anxious.

"Soweto Does Not Exist"

Johannesburg is a city which contains ghosts. In the opening pages of Mark Gevisser's (2014) autobiographical *Lost and Found in Johannesburg*, the author reflects on a childhood game in which he impersonated the role of a taxi dispatcher. With the aid of his much-loved Holmden's map book of Johannesburg he would play at plotting routes between various far-flung locations and addresses across Johannesburg. Although he became increasingly adept at such challenges, there were a series of empty spaces in the book, areas that had not been mapped, and which seemed thus to contain no inhabitants and that yet impeded his route-making activities. These apparently non-existent areas although integral to the greater Johannesburg metropolitan area, were of course, townships, of which Soweto was the most notable example. It was only after events of Soweto uprising in 1976, when this area could no longer be easily repressed from the everyday thoughts of white South Africans, that the young Gevisser came to realize that

> *Soweto wasn't there!* The huge, sprawling agglomeration of townships was a phantom in that bottom-left hand corner, in the white space below Riverlea ... where I had insouciantly plotted so many of my own fantasy suburbs; unmarked, unheeded, home to hundreds of thousands of people who commuted to the rest of the city to make it to work each day ... even though the area constituted a huge part of Johannesburg, both in population and physical size, it did not feature at all on any road maps to the city ... in some brazen example ... cartographers actually had the audacity to mark out Soweto, albeit in a solid bluish block ... before obscuring it with the inset of the downtown area. Thus does it appear, a leering dark underside to the city, its evening shadow. (2014, pp. 15–16)

In retrospect, Gevisser recalled, as a child, having heard of Alexandra ("it was that thing called a "township", that place where the Black people who worked for us would go"), even though, to all intents and purposes, "It was on another planet" (2014, p. 12). (Tellingly, he uses this phrase twice in two pages speaking about Alexandra). Not only then is it the case that Johannesburg contains the prospect of whiteness made highly visible; it also contains a kind of foreclosure of Blackness. Both such discursive operations—Soweto, and by extension, Blackness, being foreclosed, and whiteness being made unnerving self-conscious, vulnerable—give us reason to characterize Johannesburg as a place haunted by anxiety, indeed, as *the* anxious metropolis in contemporary South Africa.

Fear and Loathing Outside Luthuli House

In an earlier study on post-apartheid whiteness, one of my interviewees told me about his experience of inner-city Johannesburg. Walking near Luthuli House (the Headquarters of the country's governing African National Congress), he became aware of two Black men watching him. (A point of context: the event occurred in 2011, around the time that Julius Malema, who was then the rowdy president of the ANC's Youth League, and who had become something of a 'folk-devil for whiteness' (Falkof, 2014) due to his unrepentant views on land redistribution and unrelenting critiques of white privilege, was appearing at a disciplinary hearing for, amongst other things, humiliating a white BBC journalist who we ordered out of a press briefing.)

My interviewee described his experience of anxiety as follows:

> **Respondent:** I went to Luthuli House, during the Julius Malema [disciplinary] hearing ... I actually went to have a look ... There I am standing ... and there is this group of six guys wearing yellow T-shirts with Malema's face on it, [holding] knobkerries and sticks. They walked past and looked at me and one ... said, 'We hate all you fucking whites in South Africa.' I was with four Indian guys and one said 'It's time for us to get out of here' and so we bolted.
>
> **Interviewer:** What did you make of that. You felt ... nervous, put under threat?
>
> **Respondent:** Nervous? *Jeeslike.* I felt like a complete idiot walking down there. I couldn't feel comfortable standing on the street. They came right past me ... and I felt seriously under threat. They were armed. They could have done anything. There were two cops standing across the road and they probably wouldn't stop these guys.
>
> **Interviewer:** You think this ['We hate all you ... whites'] was said in the heat of the moment, or do you think this is how they really felt?
>
> **Respondent:** I think it is how they feel.
>
> **Interviewer:** What do you think white people think about that ... do they take [such comments] seriously?
>
> **Respondent:** I constantly hear people talking about leaving the country. Then someone in the government will say, 'Well pack your bag, we don't need you here.'

Fear of a Black Planet

A strikingly similar anecdote—even if separated by thirty or so years—is to be found in Rian Malan's (1990) *My Traitor's Heart*. This is how Malan recalls a drunken night with his Black colleague Mike, which ended up in Soweto:

> At night in Soweto, you fear what you can't see; you fear the *tsotsis*, the knifemen … It struck me that I was possibly the only white man in this vast black city and I started getting edgy … On our way into one shebeen, a disembodied black face suspended in that weird yellow light muttered something to Mike in a tribal tongue. 'He wants to know,' Mike chuckled, 'if this whitey is ripe for the picking.' Inside that shebeen, the black drinkers scowled darkly at the sight of white skin, and even Mike thought it prudent to go elsewhere … Ancient, animal unease started eating at my viscera. I slipped outside myself, and started watching Malan go through the motions … fumbling the black power handshake saying 'Hey "*bra*".' 'How you, "*bra*"' – and 'Tell me, "*bra*", is my paranoia showing?' (1990, pp. 287–88)

A little past midnight, Malan and his colleague find themselves at 'someone's Formica kitchen table, having one for the road', when

> [a] black stranger appeared in the doorway, looked me up and down, and muttered something to Mike … in a language I did not understand … I started thinking about murder and robbery, about sharpened bicycle spokes in the heart, a favourite means of dispatch in Soweto … I surged to my feet … and walked out into the menacing yellow night. A lone white man on foot in Soweto in the middle of the night … I kept my eyes down and moved fast. I passed a group of youths loitering in the surreal yellow glow; their mouths opened, and they spoke to me but no sound registered. One disembodied foot followed another … The night was as silent as outer space. I was walking on the moon … I was out of my mind with terror. (1990, p. 289)

Interestingly, at several points in his account Malan draws upon the tropes of science-fiction. He is the last (white) man in a foreign world (illuminated with a 'surreal yellow glow'); the experience of being out of (racial) place is tantamount to being on another planet; he is surrounded by others whose speech is unintelligible and whose motives are darkly opaque. A psychoanalytic injunction comes into play here: as in Freudian dream analysis, our analysis should not simply be on content but on form, on *how* what is being said is effectively said. Malan's veering into a different genre is not thus something we should overlook: racial difference—and indeed racial threat (indeed, white fragility)—is so acutely experienced that it cannot be conveyed within the conventions of journalistic prose.

The two anecdotes described above clearly mark very different moments in the history of Johannesburg. The reference to bicycle spoke killings in the Malan extract is a marker of late 1980s apartheid Johannesburg, a period when large-scale public violence featured daily in the news, and when the country seemed on the very verge of civil war. The Luthuli House example, by contrast, occurred around 30 years later, in Mandela-era post-apartheid South Africa, a historical situation which while still characterized by violence—criminal violence particularly—was not a period of large-scale civil unrest and political violence. Nonetheless, there are a series of fascinating parallels between Malan's scene and that recounted by my interviewee above. In both accounts a white man enters a Black majority space ("the black city", in Malan's terms); he is then made the object of the gaze of Black men; he battles to fathom the intentions of those who observe him; and he subsequently undergoes a vertigo of unease, experiencing the dread not merely of racial isolation, of "whiteness alone".

While it seems evident that DiAngelo's notion of white fragility applies to the above example, this conceptualization needs to be amended if is to be applied to a post-apartheid South African context (obviously very different to the United States contexts of DiAngelo's work). Her concept does not go quite far enough in grasping several facets of the phenomenon in question. Anxiety, I will argue, is a better concept with which we might explore such fraught, defensive and vulnerable experiences of whiteness in the post-apartheid context.

I make this claim for three reasons. Firstly, although DiAngelo is certainly right to highlight the factor of unconscious dispositions, she could go further to explore the imaginaries of white fragility, to attend to the narratives, and more pertinently yet, the *fantasies* that invariably attach to such experience of whiteness dislocated. Secondly, the moments of threatened and defensive whiteness that I have come across in the post-apartheid context (see also Steyn, 2004; Steyn & Foster, 2008) are typically far more pronounced than those discussed by DiAngelo. 'Fragility' doesn't do justice to the affective intensity, to the nature of the threat—or, more tellingly perhaps, the aggressiveness of response—typically elicited in such situations. A more perilous sense of ontological insecurity is invariably involved. If there is doubt as to this assertion, consider Frantz Fanon's assertion on the first page of *The Wretched of the Earth*. He writes there that "the eventuality of ... [decolonial] change is ... experienced as a terrifying future in the consciousness of ... the colonists" (2004, p. 1), a statement that is explicitly linked to "apartheid in South Africa" (2004, p. 3). Thirdly, the notion of fragility as articulated in DiAngelo's work lacks dynamism. That is to say, there is not enough consideration of what white fragility responds to, of how such anxieties might be usefully transformed, of how anxiety, as opposed to being merely reactive, might—as in the psychoanalytic clinic—be effectively worked with.[5]

'Confronting the Insect': A Paradigm of Anxiety

In the conceptualization that follows I draw inspiration from a Lacanian conceptualization of anxiety (Harari, 2001; Lacan, 2014; Soler, 2016). Let me say why. A Lacanian model is profoundly linked to issues of symbolic location, to positionality, to how a subject finds themselves relative to an Other. As such it offers us a viable means of extending the notion of white fragility precisely as experience of *dis*location. A Lacanian psychoanalytic conceptualization, moreover, is highly attuned to the realm of unconscious fantasy, to multiple dimensions of vulnerability, to ontological insecurity beyond the merely subjective, and to the prospects of change. This being said, although I draw on a psychoanalytic conceptualization of anxiety, this is not a call for an explicitly *psychological* engagement. My suggestion is that we might treat anxiety as a conceptual framework which reaches beyond the remit of the psychological, indeed, as a *psychosocial framework* with which to read a variety of literary references, fieldwork observations and experiences within post-apartheid culture.

Lacan (2014) offers a brief vignette at the beginning of his Seminar X which draws together many of the constituent elements of anxiety. This 'apologue', as he calls it, serves as a bridge between Seminar X (*Anxiety*) and his previous Seminar IX (*Identification*), a fact which stresses how crucial the latter topic (identification) is for Lacan in the various phenomena of anxiety. Lacan invokes a situation in which a dazed figure awakens to find themselves in a terrifying situation. They can feel that they are wearing a mask, although they have no idea what the features of the mask might be; in short, they don't know what they look like. Before them towers the inscrutable figure of a giant praying mantis, whose intentions are difficult to gauge, but which, at the risk of understatement, seems less than friendly. Or, in Lacan's own words, recalling the "fable" as he had previously related it:

> I pictured myself faced with another animal, a real one [...] a praying mantis. Since I didn't know what mask I was wearing, you can easily imagine that I had some reason not to feel reassured in the event that, by chance, this mask might have been just what it took to lead my partner into some error as to my identity [...] I couldn't see my own image in the enigmatic mirror of the insect's ocular globe. (Lacan, 2014, pp. 5–6)

The Kafkaesque quality of this fable should not distract us from its expository value. What the subject experiences, for Lacan, is an anxiety—or indeed, an *anguish*, to follow more recent translations of his work (see Soler, 2016)—of multiple intersecting levels. There is, firstly, what Freud (1926) would have understood as anxiety due to a real danger (*Realangst*), that is, a 'realistic' anxiety at the prospect of grievous bodily injury. (In both the above examples of white anxiety this factor is present, even it is not ultimately clear how realistic the bodily threat actually is.) There is also, secondly, anxiety at the level of personal identity, the anxiety of the ego, or, differently put, the anxiety arising from the subject's inability to summon up a familiar or self-sustaining image of themselves. It helps to recall here that in Lacan's example the subject does not know what they look like; their self-image—their sense of who they are—cannot be relied upon. (It is interesting in this respect that Malan's description entails a dissociative moment in which, as he puts it, "I slipped outside myself". It seems significant also that both Malan's situation and my interviewee felt themselves to be the only white man present.) Then there is, thirdly, anxiety at the level of symbolic inter-subjectivity, the anxiety of not knowing quite what one represents relative to the opaque desire of the Other. (It is Black men in both the above examples—potentially aggressive or unduly agitated as the case might be—who assume the place of this vexing Other.)

Anxiety thus involves the subject's difficulty of reassessment, the dilemma of trying to redefine themselves, of trying to gain a sense of both their own prospective desires and those of the Other. Importantly then, anxiety here is not a passing emotion or psychological experience. Anxiety, thus understood, cannot be limited to a circumstantial or simply intra-subjective affect; it entails an inter-subjective dimension (with the Other) and it speaks as such to the underpinnings of the subject's most crucial identifications.

In practice, of course, the above schematization breaks down: the lived experience of anxiety is difficult to confine to any of the above categories (i.e. anxiety as related to a failing self-image, anxiety as it pertains to the question of the Other's desire, etc.). And yet this schematization remains conceptually useful: it highlights that anxiety can be engendered in a wide variety of experiences—rational, bodily, relational, imaginary and so on—and its multi-dimensionality can be said to highlight precisely that the characteristically human phenomenon of anxiety is one which spills across the above conjoined registers of experience. Anxiety can as such be thought of as a reverberation of lacks—lack being coextensive with excess in Lacanian theory. (A pronounced lack of physical or ontological security gives rise, for example, to a surplus of anxious excitation.) The Lacanian conceptualization seems particularly useful in this respect: it enables us to appreciate the reverberating and thereby escalating quality of anxiety.

Taking account of this multidimensionality perhaps helps us appreciate why, in the above Luthuli House example, the research participant's sense of agitation moved so rapidly across types of anxiety. The issue of (perceived) physical danger ("I felt seriously under threat") shifted quickly to anxieties of identity and self-definition ("I felt like a complete idiot"), to the question of the desire of the Other (embodied in this situation by the imagined figure of Julius Malema), to the broader societal dilemma of what the role of whites might be in a future South Africa. There is a similar multidimensionality in Malan's case: a concern over bodily security ("bicycle spokes in the heart") is linked to a sense of ego dissociation ("I slipped outside myself"), to a sense of pronounced distance from his familiar symbolic world ("walking on the moon", "silent as outer space"). This is characteristic, I argue, of white anxiety in the post-apartheid context, experienced as it is on the associated levels of physical security, a compromised ego (in other words, the failure of one's self-image) and symbolic identity (the threat to one's historical, societal set of values). It is for this reason—the multidimensionality of the anxiety involved—that the notion of white fragility proves inadequate in the above examples. The breadth of the ontological insecurity on display exceeds what can be accommodated with the idea of fragility.

The "Lack of the Lack": Fantasy Incapacitation

The elementary sketch of anxiety provided above is not quite enough, however; to this rudimentary account we need to add the dimension of fantasy. We can understand fantasy here as that non-conscious schema of comprehension which orders the world for the subject, and that locates them, circumscribes their position, within it. It is via fantasy that the subject attains a minimal articulation of their role and subjective value in an otherwise opaque social field of competing and overlapping desires. It is fantasy, moreover, which makes the difference between a given socio-historical situation and how the subject comes to be actively (libidinally) embedded within it.

Fantasy is, furthermore, at once the compass that orients the subject in the confusing symbolic network, and a defensive formation, a filter that screens out certain realizations and organizes meaning. In fact, fantasy might be understood precisely as the subject's response to various lacks (impasses, impossibilities, imponderables) in their existential field, including, crucially, the difficulty of ever really knowing what it is the Other wants. For much of Lacan's teaching, fantasy is approached in just this way, that is, as the unconscious idea that the subject has as a way of responding to the inscrutable question of what the Other desires, and what the subject's own role is in the puzzling social reality of which they are a part. If fantasy is itself the best defense the subject has recourse to in responding to pronounced forms of lack, then we start to appreciate how incapacitating it will be for the subject to have this resource disabled. It is for this reason that Dolar (1991) says that

> [a]nxiety is the lack of the support of the lack [...] [this] "lacking support of the lack" [...] brings in the dynamics of fantasy, or the covering up of lack [...] it is the fracture of the symbolic realm – a threat of a type of symbolic death – that leads to the proximity of a second death, its subjective expression in anxiety. (1991, p. 13)

Lacan (2014) uses a similar choice of words early on in the *Seminar*: "anxiety [...] has to be conceived of at a duplicated level, as the failing of the support that lack provides" (p. 53). Hence the famous Lacanian aphorism repeated throughout the *Seminar*: the idea that anxiety is "the lack of the lack." How might we render this idea in more straightforward terms? Perhaps as follows: anxiety arises when the conditions supporting the *possibility of desire* are themselves lacking. Desire here, importantly, connotes not simply desirousness, but desire precisely—as we have seen—as the desire-of-the-Other, desire as a mode of "cognitive mapping," as a means of locating one's place in the symbolic network, and as a means anchoring the social and subjective identifications that allow the subject to experience themselves, and their surrounding world, as coherent.

From a Lacanian standpoint, then, what engenders anxiety in the subject is not so much an experience of deprivation—the loss, say, of some or other object—but rather a type of suffocating lack that undercuts the subjective, symbolic and/or mortal viability of the desiring subject as such. Lacan is unusually clear on this point: "Anxiety isn't about the loss of the object, but its presence" (p. 54). We can appreciate, then, how in anxiety the absence of lack (Lacan's "lack of the lack") is coterminous with the presence of an intrusive, libidinally excessive object. The presence of such an object cannot but strike Freudians as an odd amendment to Freud's theorizations of anxiety, one constant of which is that anxiety—unlike fear—has no readily identifiable object. Lacan offers a double negation as a way of bridging Freudian theorizations with his own conceptualizations: "anxiety is not without an object". Or, in a variation of the same: the subject of anxiety is "not without having it" (p. 85). That is to say: there *is* an object in anxiety, but it is an object in a very particular sense.

Margarita Palacios (2013) stresses that in Lacan's conceptualization, the object in states of anxiety is not the empirical object that we experience through our senses, but is rather the *object a*,

> which by "not being there" allows the phenomenological experience to take place: desire and knowledge are possible only because of the exclusion of the "real" [...]. The open space, the disjuncture of language and being, puts desire in motion; "*a*" in this sense [...] by not being there [...] puts desire and meaning in motion [...] [for Lacan] this constitutional lack is covered – and secured – by fantasy and experienced as [...] desire. (p. 50)

Palacios probes the issue further, asking why the *object a*—a type of absence incarnated, an absence made object—should be related to the experience of anxiety? Her answer is that

> anxiety signals a presence, this means that instead of the necessary lack that puts desire in motion, the subject is "asphyxiated" by the proximity of the

> object causes of desire. Anxiety signals a failure in symbolic reality, a disappearance of the fantasy support of desire. (p. 51)

Anxiety thus points to "the possibility of the void being closed, the drying up of desire, the failure of fantasy" (Palacios, 2013, p. 53). *Jouissance* is also a factor here, for fantasy not only arranges the subject's world, endows their experience of psychical reality with a degree of consistency, but also acts as a barrier that differentiates desire from *jouissance*. Anxiety is at the same time, then, reaction and signal: it is both the result of the incapacitation of fantasy and a warning of an influx of traumatic enjoyment.

So, while anxiety is indeed related to the experience of something being "too much", a "too close" presence of the object, the crucial error to avoid is that of prioritizing the "actual" empirical object as itself the cause of anxiety. Anxiety, to recap, is the failure of the fantasy which covers up lack, that orders the subject's world, explains their role with the world, and which dictates what and how they desire. In the absence of such a fantasy, the subject encounters an abyss of identity, the prospect of symbolic death (to again cite Dolar (1991)), to which they typically respond—as in the case of the Terblanche Delport outlined above—in ways that are as aggressive as they are seemingly disproportionate. It is this factor, of anxiety understood precisely as fantasy incapacitated, that provides the most apt psychoanalytic explanation for the vitriol that Delport encountered. The ferocity of these responses, the nerve touched by his mention of white suicide, is a sure sign that Delport's adversaries had been confronted with imaginary castration, that is, with the threatened extinction of their most cherished identificatory images along with that of the most valued symbolic and existential meanings underlying their investment in whiteness.

One further point should be added here. When fantasy seizes up, the consistency of the subject's psychical reality is compromised, and they subsequently experience a troubling excessive (non)object, an anxious incarnation of *object a*. This is the direct result of "the lack of the lack". Here, it helps to recall that the emergence of an intrusive asphyxiating (non) object (*object a*) *is* coextensive with the collapse of desire (Palacios, 2013). The elevation of what might otherwise be an unimportant object to the position of the monstrous (non)object of anxiety is evident in all the examples cited above. We see such ((non)object/*object a*) embodiments in the threatening Julius Malema supporters mentioned by my interviewee, in the "black stranger" and the ghastly unearthly nighttime environs of

Soweto recounted by Malan, and, presumably, in the figure of Delport himself. To add the necessary Lacanian qualification: the disconcerting quality of such (non)objects has less to do with any of their inherent properties than with where they occur, with how they disturb the subject's fantasmatic arrangement of the world. Anxiety, then, is less about an object per se than about a crushing experience of "out of placeness," an idea which of course resonates with my earlier suggestion that DiAngelo's (2011, 2018) idea of white fragility could be read as a theory of dislocation.

Crucially, none of the above is to make excuses for—or justify—white anxiety or the racist sentiments that so often accompany it. To adopt an apologetic or defensive stance would be imply that anxiety is necessarily a negative or detrimental phenomenon. Clinically, this is certainly not the case. If anything, we could argue that there is a need for *more* white anxiety in the post-apartheid context. Why? Well, we might ask a related question: why should the notion of anxiety benefit us at all, analytically? One answer is to be found in psychoanalyst Bruce Fink's thoughts on the value of anxiety in clinical treatments:

> Anxiety plays a role in clinical work in that when it manifests itself it signals to the clinician that he or she is getting close to something, and that interpretation could really have a truly significant effect at that moment. It indicates something about *object a* [i.e. that which causes desire] ... that it is operating at that point, that there's a concern with loss, a question of castration. A treatment in which anxiety doesn't present itself is almost unthinkable; if you never arouse any anxiety in your patients, you probably will never get anywhere .... Anxiety always appears at the moment where there's something repressed – the repressed is about to appear in some way or is in play, being touched upon in some way. (2014, p. 247)

We might say then, speaking figuratively, that there is some value in anxiety, in the Kafkaesque dilemma (and/or Lacanian scenario) of confronting the insect.

Armageddon Time

Anxiety is always a temporal relation, certainly insofar as it entails a future-oriented sense of anticipation or dread. Moreover, anxiety is also, as Freud (1926) insists, a signal, a warning; it is not itself a traumatic experience, but rather the nervous expectation of such an experience (as in Crapanzano's (1985) equation—discussed in the previous chapter—of anxiety in the white South African context with the state of *waiting for something to happen*). I note this not simply to contrast with the more static notion of white fragility, but also to suggest that such a future-oriented temporality lends itself to the production of fantasmatic narratives. Hence, also, the importance of the state of anticipation—or of suspension, interruption, scansion—for Lacanian psychoanalysis: what cannot be known with any degree of certainty is fertile ground for the ruminations of the unconscious.

It is of interest that this aspect—the future-directed temporality of anxiety—is so frequently linked with fantasies of extinction and/or erasure in the empirical field. This combination makes for a virtual sub-genre sub-genre in contemporary South African literature. In his discussion of autobiographical South African writing, Murray (2013) identifies alarmist narratives of 'the future unwanted' as one of the basic categories of stories that white post-apartheid South Africans tell about themselves. These narratives are

> futurist, eschatological tales that warn of impending doom. They exemplify a dystopian, apocalyptic discourse of fear, anxiety, and disavowal. They operate as powerful vehicles for the politics of negation – a dismissive repudiation of the transformative, progressive consequences of the transition to democracy. (2013, 175)

Such accounts vary in tone, from self-aggrandizing to the self-deprecating, and in affective range from cautionary tale to full-blown apocalyptic vision. Clinically, the imperative here is clear: we should remain particularly attentive if a patient wishes to dwell on reveries concerning the aftermath of their life. From a psychoanalytic perspective, such speculative thoughts—once encouraged and further articulated—make for rich material; imaginaries of demise have much to tell us about the fantasmatic preoccupations of a particular individual or community, about their narcissistic myths, their entrenched fears, their wishful utopias and ideals, about their most intense libidinal investments. Each of these considerations has, in turn, much to tell us about their identifications—conscious and unconscious—and about the prospects of changing such identifications.

Back then to Malan. His journalism after *My Traitor's Heart* (1990), has—unsurprisingly perhaps—been characterized by a pessimistic vision of South Africa's future, and a deep anxiety about the role, if any, of whites and Afrikaners in the country. There is an 'end times' quality to many of the scenes and situations that Malan describes, as two of the chapter titles in his recent collection *Resident Alien* make abundantly clear: 'The last Afrikaner', 'Houses going cheap in doomed country'. An effective but more obviously parodic counterpart to Malan's imagery is that of visual artist Anton Kannemeyer (2010), who uses a comic book style to depict scenes of what he refers to as 'apartheid apocalypse', in which we bear witness to the mortification of various ideals of white apartheid South Africa. In an image 'N is for nightmare', for example, he depicts a Black domestic worker serving up the head of his dead white former master. The anxiety Malan expresses—and this holds true also of *My Traitor's Heart*—concerns not only a desperate sense of non-relevance, but a suspicion that the broader significance of white South African history might itself be altogether erased.

In the postscript to *Resident Alien*, a collection of writings largely centered on his experiences of Johannesburg, Malan likens South Africa's post-apartheid future to a period in the history of ancient Britain. After the Romans abandoned the country, the roads, villas, and systems of social organization that they had put in place were plunged into the Dark Ages by the savage Celts. In much the same way, Malan laments, "Johannesburg as we know it will vanish" (2011, 338). He continues:

> Many centuries hence … Africans [will struggle] to decipher the crumbling texts of a race that once lived there, planting cornfields … splitting atoms, and making the trains run on time … Afrikaans will be the ghost that rattles its chains in the depths of some new African tongue … The good that white men did will be acknowledged, the evil forgotten. (2011, p. 338)

The cultural and racial narcissism here, like the self-pitying image of white (Afrikaner) extinction, seems obvious enough. (Here, incidentally, the difference between Kannemeyer and Malan is writ large: Kannemeyer's (2010) portrayals of white anxiety involve a healthy dose of ironic distance; no such ironic distance exists in Malan.) It could be argued—if unconvincingly—that Malan is attempting to build narrative tension by a deliberate conjuring of historical images of Africa as the de-civilizing Heart of Darkness. For many readers of Malan, interest in his work stops here, when the racism of the text and its apparent colonial-era associations become unavoidable. However, rather than foregoing the text at this point or treating it simply as symptomatic of the racism of its context, we should,

I think, persist. Malan's images of racial apocalypse are perhaps more ambivalent than they at first appear. We should treat this description in the same way one treats fantasies in the clinical context, that is, not only as illusory (and, in this case, racist) flights of fancy, but more dynamically, that is, as occasioned by and responding to psychical processes of castration, identification, and possibly, *denied* identification.

A lengthy section of *My Traitor's Heart* entitled 'A root in the arid ground' is devoted to the story of Neil and Creina Alcock, two white South Africans who turned their backs on white apartheid privilege and attempted to make a success of farming in the unforgiving conditions of Msinga. Here Malan once again deploys the tropes of the Dark Continent in ways which arguably both animate and agitate racist stereotypes. In the opening pages of this essay, Malan enjoins his reader to join him on an expedition to Msinga, evoking thus the narrative device of the imagined journey to evoke unease and dread in the reader:

> Some ten miles beyond the last white town, you cross the border between the First and Third Worlds, between white South Africa and black KwaZulu ... You know you are coming into a different country, a different world. The white centreline vanishes, and the road itself starts rearing and plunging, like a turbulent river rushing toward a waterfall. (1991, p. 339)

Now while this perspective, that of the well-intentioned explorer in the non-white world, cannot but imply a colonial standpoint, there is more than just this to be discovered here. The Alcocks, Malan informs us,

> spent two decades living among Africans, like Africans, trying to undo some of the hard done by apartheid. They lived in mud huts and shat in holes in the ground. They washed their clothes and bodies in the Tugela River ... [They] were always dusty and dishevelled. They endured fire ants in their armpits and rats in their beds, unbearable heat in summer and biting cold in winter. They were as ragged as the black peasants among whom they worked. (1991, pp. 342–343)

The above characterization of Africans and "black peasants" is lamentable, to say the least. Nonetheless, if we persist interesting material comes to the fore. As intimated above, a psychoanalytic consideration of fantasies of demise can be fruitful in revealing (unconscious) identifications. The above view of life beyond the "white centerline" seems to perform a kind of demise, presenting as it does, a journey beyond whiteness. Such imaginaries of demise can be particularly useful in exploring latent identifications, identifications of the 'unthought known' variety. Anxiety here might be conceptualized as a barrier that keeps the subject from exploring prospective identifications, or perhaps more importantly, identifications that—in a partial and perhaps unconscious sense—a subject may not yet realize they have already made.

If the abiding concern of much of Malan's writing is with the question of what will become of whites and, more particularly, white Afrikaners, in a future South Africa, then his work also offers—despite the dystopian fatalism he seems so prone to—a possible answer: something different, something Other. This is a something that cannot quite yet be imagined, although it is, by the same token, a something requiring that prior constituent identifications be left behind, laid to rest in a way perhaps not too dissimilar to the notion of a suicide of symbolic values.

So, if anxiety for Freud and Lacan is often a signal—a signal, moreover, that (unlike other affects) *does not lie*—then one value of the concept as it occurs, clinically, is that it serves to indicate (to signal) the prospective end of an ego, the potential demise of a series of identifications. This, to be sure, is a frightening situation, one in which dread comes palpably to the fore. In this respect the above descriptive of how the imaginaries of castration, of subjective and racial extinction are conjoined, juxtaposed, overlapping, seems apt. And yet the *potentiality* of anxiety must be kept in mind here; white anxiety—unlike the notion of white fragility—entails the prospect of transformation. We might reiterate this point by noting that to speak of the end of an ego (or, of the end a series of identifications) is not to speak simply of death, but of an event in which something new may emerge by virtue of a given imaginary/symbolic demise. So, even within the context of heightened anxiety, many of the above examples also contain a concession—even if, admittedly of a frequently fearful or reactionary sort—that a new form of identification is the subject of unconscious rumination.

For many the above excursion into the fantasy terrain of white anxiety will have proved too much simply by virtue of the racism it forces one to confront. And it is true: to explore this terrain is to find oneself amongst many of the most persistent historical tropes of white racism. Any yet, there is a sense in which this, trawling through racist fantasy, remains an important political task. We might again draw inspiration from the psychoanalytic clinic. Isn't this, after all, what the clinical practice psychoanalysis aims for: to elicit fantasy, to encourage the analysand to give voice to what is otherwise unacceptable, to put words to what cannot otherwise be said, and do so in this way that guide the slow process of moving beyond the *jouissance*-laden domain of fantasy? The idea, after all, is that by working through such material, 'hearing it out', draining it of enjoyment and thereby exhausting it, we might decrease its hold on the analysand such that they are less beholden to it. One outcome of such a process, should it be successful, is that what had seemed unthinkable, what had elicited myriad defensive reactions ('the end of whiteness') might, in due course, become manageable, ordinary, even banal.

In a post-script to *Resident Alien*, Malan returns to the theme of a future 'post-whites' Johannesburg. "Johannesburg as we know it will vanish" he says, before adding: "visitors to this New Jerusalem will encounter something presently inconceivable – Africans … struggling to decipher the crumbling texts of a race that once lived here" (2011, p. 338). While, once again, this fantasmatic rendering does not escape the hubris of white narcissism, it does present us with a view of a post-whiteness future about which Malan remarks: "I scheme it will be quite lekker" ["I think it'll be pretty great"] (2011, 338).[6]

Another Scene, Another District, or: Neil Blomkamp as Reader of Kafka

The scene is thus set for the single most riveting text of post-apartheid dystopian science fiction: Neil Blomkamp's (2009) *District 9*. While the name of the film would not have been particularly resonant for an international audience, for South Africans the title cannot but invoke District 6, the historically cosmopolitan, racially diverse, working-class area of Cape Town with a large immigrant population that was effectively erased—subjected to forced removals—by the apartheid government. These removals followed depictions of the area as a crime-ridden, dangerous slum whose various forms of interracial interaction necessarily bred conflict. *District 9* recasts many of these historical features, projecting them from South Africa's apartheid past to the mega-city context of contemporary Johannesburg, where the above characterizations are present in hugely amplified proportions.[7]

Much has been written on the film emphasizing its relationship to apartheid-era race relations and emphasizing the abject quality of the insectoid alien others. Let us consider a representative, sympathetic engagement with the film:

> *District 9* … was subversive, intelligent, amusing and felt authentic … By transplanting the apartheid logic and culture in a speculative future Joburg populated by giant … prawns … who operated as the perennial 'other', Blomkamp found a way for South Africans to mediate on their history from a distance and paradoxically, through the lens of the future. This distance proved ideologically useful to us; it was like a mirror that allowed us to see how the culture of a prejudice based on difference had been passed from generation to generation, like a cursed heirloom. (Corrigal, 2012)

While I agree with much of what Corrigall maintains here, her comments focus more on the past than on the future of whiteness in South Africa. It seems to me that by nature of the film's genre (science fiction), we should equally consider how it anticipates a future, and, more particularly, future forms of whiteness. We can read the film as responding to the psychical-political-existential dilemmas running through all the forms of post-apartheid white anxiety mentioned above, namely: What must I, the white South African, do—or become—in this post-apartheid era? What, furthermore, is to become of us whites (and white Afrikaners) in this 'strange place' where we can no longer rely on the defining values and symbolic identities which we benefitted from in the era of apartheid? Wikus van der Merwe, the unfortunate hero of *District 9*, who of course begins to change into one of the alien 'prawns' so reviled and feared by the humans in the film, seems at first to offer us little hope. In fact, the fate of Wikus seems simply to replay, at an exaggerated inter-galactic level, one of the great fears of colonial anxiety—that of miscegenation.

Here, I think, we should exercise caution before reading the film as merely recycling the racist tropes and figures of apartheid and deploying them in a future context. Like Malan's writings, *District 9* certainly has not shaken off the colonial themes (in this case, of sub-human otherness, of miscegenation, etc.), and yet it stages a type of white demise that is surely a precondition for foregoing subjective investments in whiteness, for considering an unbecoming of whiteness.

Or, to take a different tack: what occurs if we approach Blomkamp not merely as revisiting apartheid, but as a reader of Kafka? The literary reference to Kafka's (2009) famous story *The Metamorphosis*, about a man who becomes an insect, seems difficult to deny ("When Gregor Samsa woke one morning from uneasy dreams, he found himself transformed into some kind of monstrous vermin" (Kafka, 2009, p. 26)). Similarly, it is curious that the emblem Lacan uses in his paradigmatic example of anxiety—the human-sized prey mantis—is so close to the scenario envisaged by Blomkamp, in which Wikus is suddenly tasked with the role of negotiating with the inscrutable and dangerous insectoid aliens.

I mentioned above that in Lacan's estimation, anxiety and questions of subjective and social identification are inextricably linked. Anxiety in its distinctively human form arises most acutely not simply as an isolated issue of physical security or impeding death, but when the coordinates of personal, subjective (imaginary) identification and sociological and historical (symbolic) identification are simultaneously threatened with erasure. It is the precariousness of existence as experienced at these multiple levels which characterizes the angst, dread or nausea described by existential thinkers as varied as Kierkegaard, Camus, and Sartre. This is why Kafka's parable is so disturbing: the experience of becoming an insect is not merely that of death nor that of psychological or symbolic transformation; it is that of existing at a wholly different ontological level, of completely unbecoming one's (physical, psychological, symbolic) self. The exaggerated otherness of Blompkamp's aliens seems to affirm the point: these insectoid figures—so far from the 'human' aliens of Spielberg's *E.T.* and *Close Encounters of the Third Kind*—are precisely impossible to identify with. To become one of the prawns is to sever all links with one's previous existence (a fact nicely dramatized by the film's subplot in which the pre-infection Wikus is due to be married to his sweetheart, the daughter of his boss). Wikus-as-prawn will be changed in his very species-being; he will have completed the process of fully unbecoming what he once was.

And this is why one might read the film as offering us an important ethical opportunity, one which unexpectedly mirrors the controversial gesture of white racial suicide suggested by Terblanche Delport (2016). Delport's rhetorical and deliberately provocative suggestion is perhaps not as counter-intuitive or crazy as it at first sounds. Delport took his white audience to the threshold of symbolic extinction, to a proposed 'end of whiteness'. In psychoanalytic terms, Delport offered his audience the opportunity to contemplate the castration of whiteness. This is, admittedly, a risky strategy—but perhaps a necessary one. How so? It is, surely, the gesture of giving up what one is—the shedding of narcissistic investments, symbolic and fantasmatic identities—that proves a necessary first step to becoming what one is not, but what become. This is the transformative potential of anxiety that clinicians work so hard to facilitate. It is a potential that can also be discerned—however fleetingly—in the instances of white anxiety discussed above: the potentiality that a new—and hitherto unthinkable—form of identification is being unconsciously processed, is beginning to take root.

Notes

1. In an article entitled 'Whiteness without apartheid', Achille Mbembe (2007) has offered an insightful analysis of how white privilege has been secured despite the various structural and political changes brought about since the end of apartheid:

   > To protect white privilege, boundaries were created that took the form of laws, customs and traditions. A *racist ethos*, a deeply embedded racist *habitus* constantly helped to justify whites' loss of feeling for human fellowship with blacks. This is how white privilege came to be seen as an entitlement that was hardly ever contested. Indeed, whites' ability over more than a century to pass out to succeeding generations the spoils of racial discrimination in monetary or property value, banking practices, housing markets, educational resources, cultural capital, insider networks, good jobs and media representations – this has something to do with current levels of racial inequality and black poverty.

2. Yancy has returned to this theme. Consider the following remarks, offered in a (forthcoming) dialogue with Sheldon George, in respect of what it would take to "change white enjoyment of Black death":

   > [it would] involve something traumatic and unnerving vis-à-vis whiteness. It will involve the death of whiteness. The death of whiteness must involve real change, which is not the same as engaging in processes to rehabilitate whiteness ... What I am proposing here... will involve the collapse of processes of white worlding, and white identity. It means the end of the white horizon in terms of which what appears within the structure of whiteness ... no longer appears... [This] means the collapse of white intelligibility, the nullification of a white episteme or a white regime of knowledge production ... white enjoyment of Black death will not be ritualistically necessary given the death of whiteness ... Whiteness, in short, must starve. It must atrophy, waste away.

3. SA-news.com announced that Delport had "publically called for the genocide of White South Africans" and lamented how unfortunate it was that he had "not been accused of hate speech". The BondStaat Facebook page (BondStaat, n.d.) likewise reported the event, alleging that Delport had claimed that "White South Africans should commit suicide and die out without having children", before adding, "The genocidal hatemonger's details are below if you would like to "discuss" his very public opinion with him".
4. While Johannesburg is certainly not alone in this (border crossing) feature, it does feature—on a larger scale than anywhere else in the country—jarring

juxtapositions between the near adjacent spaces of white suburban affluence and township life, as the disparities between Sandton and Alexandra, Fourways and Diepsloot, and to a somewhat lesser extent Johannesburg South and Soweto, make abundantly clear (Harber, 2011).

5. Differently put, white fragility often seems a somewhat static notion (to be fragile is, presumably, to remain fragile; there is little scope to adapt, to become robust, etc.). DiAngelo's (2011) conceptualization does not, as such, particularly lend itself to an understanding of transformation.
6. This suggests a prospective, if potentially perilous, political strategy for the future. Instead of immediately censoring racist fantasies, shutting them down—which, in the majority of cases, and certainly in public fora, remains crucial given the degree of hate-speech potentially involved—might it be possible to drain such fantasies of their *jouissance*? Might it be possible, moreover, to intervene within various of the narrative components of such fantasies, and to do so as a means of rerouting the subject of whiteness, as a way of facilitating the unbecoming of whiteness? This, admittedly, is to risk extrapolating from the ethical containment of the psychoanalytic clinic to the spheres of public discourse and social media, spheres which seek to heighten rather than to contain the *jouissance* and ideological utility of such fantasies.
7. While in the film District 9 is a district of Johannesburg, one could argue that District 9 is itself a metonymic extension of the city itself. At once foreign (indeed, itself alien) to many US viewers—a glaring contrast from the gleaming-then-crumbling skyscrapers of most generic disaster films—Blompkamp's Johannesburg is a city perfectly suited to the abjection of the situation it depicts.

References

Ahmed, S. (2007). A phenomenology of whiteness. *Feminist Theory, 8*(2), 149–168.

Blomkamp, N. (dir.) (2009). *District 9*. Wingnut Pictures/Tristar.

BondStaat Facebook page: https://www.facebook.com/bondstaat/posts/white-south-africans-should-commit-suicide-and-die-out-without-having-children-t/1054435757981307/

Bonilla-Silva, E. (2017). *Racism Without Racists: Colorblind Racism and the Persistence of Racial Inequality in America*. Rowman & Littlefield.

Bonilla-Silva, E., Goar, C., & Embrick, D. G. (2006). When whites flock together: The social psychology of white habitus. *Critical Sociology, 32*(2–3), 229–253.

Bourdieu, P. (1993). *The Field of Cultural Production*. Columbia University Press.

Corrigal, M. (2012). SA's forward-looking Neil Blomkamp is stuck in the past. *Sunday Independent*, 6 April.

Crapanzano, V. (1985). *Waiting: The Whites of South Africa*. Granada.

Delport, T. (2016). Personal communication. Email, 16 March.
DiAngelo, R. (2011). White fragility. *International Journal of Critical Pedagogy, 3*(3), 54–70.
DiAngelo, R. (2018). *White Fragility*. Beacon Press.
Dolar, M. (1991). "I shall be with you on your wedding night": Lacan and the uncanny. *October* 58 (Autumn), 5–23.
Durrheim, K., & Dixon, J. (2014). *Racial Encounter: The Social Psychology of Contact and Desegregation*. Routledge.
Dyer, R. (1997). *White*. Routledge.
Falkof, N. (2014). Talking the (white) talk; walking the (white) walk. *Daily Maverick*, 19 June.
Falkof, N. (2016). *The End of Whiteness*. Jacanna.
Fanon, F. (2004). *The Wretched of the Earth*. Grove Press.
Fine, M. (1997). Witnessing Whiteness. In M. Fine, L. Weiss, C. Powell, & L. Wong (Eds.), *Off White: Readings on Race, Power and Society* (pp. vii–xii). Routledge.
Fink, B. (2014). *Against Understanding, Volume 2: Cases and Commentary in a Lacanian Critique*. Routledge.
Frankenberg, R. (1993). *The Social Construction of Whiteness: White Women, Race Matters*. University of Minnesota Press.
Freud, S. (1926). Inhibition, Symptoms and Anxiety. In *The Standard Edition of the Complete Psychological Works of Sigmund Freud* (Vol. 20, pp. 75–174).
Gevisser, M. (2014). *Lost and Found in Johannesburg*. Jonathan Ball.
Haffajee, F. (2015). *What if there were No Whites in South Africa?* Pan Macmillan.
Harari, R. (2001). *Lacan's Seminar on 'Anxiety'*. Other Press.
Harber, A. (2011). *Diepsloot*. Jonathan Ball.
Kafka, F. (2009). The Metamorphosis. In *The Metamorphosis and Other Stories*. Oxford University Press.
Kannemeyer, A. (2010). *Alphabet of Democracy*. Jacana Media.
Lacan, J. (2014). In J-A. Miller (Ed.), *Anxiety: The Seminar of Jacques Lacan, Book X* (A. R. Price, Trans.). Polity Press.
Malan, R. (1990). *My Traitor's Heart*. Vintage.
Malan, R. (2011). *Resident Alien*. Jonathan Ball.
Mbembe, A. (2007). *Whiteness without apartheid: The limits of racial freedom*. Retrieved from https://www.opendemocracy.net/en/whiteness_without_apartheid_the_limits_of_racial_freedom/
Mbembe, A., & Nuttall, S. (2008). Introduction: Afropolis. In S. Nuttall & A. Mbembe (Eds.), *Johannesburg: The Elusive Metropolis*. Wits University Press.
Murray, M. (2013). *Commemorating and Forgetting: Challenges for the New South Africa*. University of Minnesota Press.
Ngo, H. (2017). *The Habits of Racism: A Phenomenology of Racism and Racialization*. Lexington.

Palacios, M. (2013). *Radical Sociality: On Disobedience, Violence and Belonging*. Palgrave.

Sithole, T. (2024). *Black X: Liberatory Thought in Azania*. Wits University Press.

Soler, C. (2016). *Lacanian Affects: The Function of Affect in Lacan's Work* (B. Fink, Trans.). Routledge.

Steyn, M. E. (1998). White Identity in Context in a Personal Narrative. In T. K. Nakayama & J. N. Martin (Eds.), *Whiteness: The Communication of Social Identity* (pp. 264–278). Sage.

Steyn, M. E. (2004). Rehabilitating a whiteness disgraced: Afrikaner white talk in post-apartheid South Africa. *Communications Quarterly, 52*(2), 143–169.

Steyn, M. E., & Foster, D. (2008). Repertoires for talking white: Resistant whiteness in post-apartheid South Africa. *Ethnic and Racial Studies, 31*(1), 25–51.

Yancy, G. (2012). *Look, A White! Philosophical Essays on Whiteness.* Temple University Press.

Yancy, G. (2018). *Backlash What Happens When we Talk Honestly about Racism in America*. Rowman & Littlefield.

CHAPTER 4

Reflections on a Scene of Attack

Abstract This chapter describes a series of attacks that I was subjected to after delivering a lecture on the topic of 'white anxiety'. The focus of the attacks concerned the notion of the 'end of whiteness', and the idea, discussed at length in the foregoing chapter, of a type of 'white suicide'. The chapter cites indicative extracts from the barrage of hate messages. The over-arching purpose of the attacks was to consolidate an oppositional hard-right political identity—often, but not always of a generally White Nationalist sort—and, accordingly, to stoke a politics of grievance, by linking together a series of maligned signifiers associated with a progressive or leftist position. What was less expected was the sheer extent of the 'unreconstructed' types of racism and antisemitism on display. I try to understand this via the discursive trope of the 'race traitor' and by means of the idea of performative offensiveness, that is, the demonstrative attempt to offend, by explicitly saying and relishing that which is typically prohibited. Oddly enough, despite that many implied threats were issued, and a great many unpleasant things were wished upon me and my family, there was still a suggestion that I might be rescued, retrieved from 'woke indoctrination'. I close with a few critical reflections on my own position of enunciation.

Keywords Antisemitism • Online attacks • Performative offensiveness • Race traitor • Racism • White Nationalism • Wokeness

D. Hook, *Whiteness at the Abyss*, The Palgrave Lacan Series,
https://doi.org/10.1007/978-3-031-78509-2_4

On 12 June 2021 I delivered a formal lecture on the topic discussed in the previous chapter, that of 'White Anxiety', to the American Association for Psychoanalysis in Social Work (AAPCSW). The lecture was part of a series of talks focused on the theme of 'Deconstructing Whiteness to an Anti-Racist Clinical Practice'. Several weeks after I had delivered lecture, the zoom recording was—with my permission—made available on the AAPCSW's website—I had, naïvely, thought that few people apart from members of AAPCSW would find the remarks of any interest. A few days later, after a trolling expedition, comments that I had made in the talk were cut from the recording and distributed widely online, with the obvious intent to cause outrage and condemnation. The resultant Twitter storm was exacerbated by media attention and by an online Fox News story (Colton, 2021). The contentious material focused on the notion of the 'end of whiteness', and the idea, discussed at length in the foregoing chapter, of 'white suicide'. This chapter focusses on this scene of attack. More specifically, it identifies and explores a series of themes and discursive strategies that predominated in the barrage of hate messages I received between August and November of 2021.

The attacks, which took on a far more orchestrated form than I would have anticipated, assumed a variety of forms: threatening letters; calls; emails; tweets and exponentially multiplying retweets; doxing (online publication of personal details, images of my family); attempts at hacking my email account; comments by online trolls; and calls for the termination of my employment. As I have come to understand, campaigns of this sort are often well organized. The senior administrative assistant in my department at Duquesne University, who regrettably bore the brunt of many offensive and threatening calls, remarked that there were certain times when dozens of calls were made in rapid succession and other times of relative silence. It was not just the timing of the calls, but the similarity of what was said ("We're coming for him") that suggested to her that they had been coordinated. The same was true of the timing of emails: I would be subjected to a barrage of emails all within a few minutes of one another and then a pause of a few hours. It was as if a rudimentary set of protocols were in place; many of those calling and emailing me seemed well-practiced in the genre of the anxiety-inducing message: invariably obscene and threatening, but not so declarative of violent intent that it might open them up to possible police attention.[1]

Such campaigns of intimidation are not, unfortunately, new—they are, today, the modus operandi adopted by those who wish to vilify and intimidate scholars with an ostensibly left-wing agenda. Nonetheless, it seems important to examine the particularity of both the contents and discursive form of the attacking messages I received, even though this campaign of intimidation was of a relatively modest scale, certainly so compared to the extent of what colleagues such as George Yancy (Yancy, 2018), Lara Sheehi and Donald Moss (Moss, 2021; see also Zeavin's (2022) account of the attacks on Moss) have been exposed to in recent years.[2]

A few methodological remarks are in order. Given that the barrage of messages involved was simply too large—and at times, too disturbing—to grapple with, I resolved simply to keep a record of the attacking emails received, such that I might refer to them later (it proved too difficult to keep a record of the spiraling array of tweets and retweets). I forwarded all the emails that I received at the time—in many instances without reading them—to my colleagues Anna Kreienberg and Benjamin Strosberg, who created a corpus comprised of this material. I read hardly any of the of the tweets—Twitter was invariably the means through which the worst of the threatening and derogatory messages were conveyed—although Anna, Benjamin and my partner did, so as to monitor for 'actionable threats' to myself or my family.

There are lessons to be learnt following a close reading of the emails, lessons going beyond what many colleagues noted when the attack campaign was in full swing: that my original talk powerfully elicited precisely what it had attempted to analyze: the aggressive defensiveness of white fragility and/or white anxiety (DiAngelo, 2018; Hook, 2020a). My analysis of the material, which combines thematic, discourse analytic and—as seems justified in this case—personal reflections, yielded a series of core themes: (1) an open-ended chain of maligned signifiers, (2) the role of the messages in consolidating identity, (3) performative offensiveness, (4) support from the Twitter-Sphere, (5) perverse intimidations, (6) accusations/denials/expressions of racism, (7) the race-traitor as ideological dilemma, (8) antisemitism, and (9) aggressive cordiality. I close by reflecting on legitimate criticisms voiced within the emails and upon my own enunciative position.

A Chain of Maligned Signifiers

Let us begin with a representative example of the attacking emails, one which combines many of the basic reoccurring themes:

Sent: Sunday, September 5, 2021 5:08:13 PM

Subject: [External] Kill Yourself Instead, Psychotic Democrat Nazi Professor From Hell, Derek Hook

You deranged piece of Democrat Nazi garbage, Derek Scumbag Hook, you need to kill yourself. Do it now, you fucking loser. Take your white guilt bullshit, you woke mentally disturbed piece of shit and get off my planet. ...

No white person should feel even the slightest guilt about the lowlife [n-word] felon. They are beneath us and also should be dead. ... no white person should feel any guilt about them. It is your lowlife Black Lives Don't Matter For Shit Terrorist Organization that deserves for every member to be exterminated and suffer the most painful and excruciating deaths possible.

And you Derek Hook deserve the same fate. ... You deserve getting your head chopped off ... If you have a gun, blow your brains out. If you don't, go to the top of a large building and jump off of it. ... you are a malignant cancer that needs to leave the Earth ASAP!!!!!

Aside from the horror B-movie schlock of the email's description of a "Psychotic Democrat Nazi Professor From Hell"—there were numerous examples of unintentional humor in such emails—what is immediately apparent here is how the above attack allies itself with a hard-right political stance, one which opposes not only "Democrat...garbage", "white guilt bullshit", but woke-ness, Black Lives Matter, etc., etc. The circle of designated adversaries grew increasingly large as the emails came in, coming to including, amongst others: "screaming liberals", "revenge politicians...the same as Ilhan Omar", "democRats", "woketard parasites", "woke academics", "libtards", those focused "on the demonization of white culture", "Marxist parasites", "communists", those who are "Vaxx compliant", and, predictably, proponents of Critical Race Theory (the "CRT paradigm"), which, as one attacker informed me, "teaches African Americans to see themselves as a victim which they are not". There was rarely simply one target of abuse; the emails invariably involved—the first basic finding of my analysis—an open-ended chain of hated signifiers which could be rearranged in a variety of ways.

An entire "culture of wokeness" was being targeted: "you're part of a culture that is tearing this country apart with ideas, concepts, teachings...hate is generated by so many people in "learned" positions". The malign influence of liberal universities was frequently noted: "You and other insane professors are the reason our education system has turned into an indoctrination camp for young minds". Messages stressed, for example, "the stupidity of higher learning", that "universities are only interested in preparing students to become radical activists", warning that "when the great backlash against leftist indoctrination finally arrives, it will be people like you who suffer the most—and rightly so". I was attacked particularly insofar as I was a representative of the "woketard parasite dumbass bitch whores and bastard sons of whores in academia".

An aligned mode of attack contended that I was one of the "perfect pseudo-intellectual idiots for a post-national oligarchy...bent on destroying traditional mainstream American culture". While it did not occur frequently enough to count as a dominant theme, a significant number of the emails drew on conspiratorial narratives: "We all realize that our government, big technology and monopolies have promoted [the idea of] "racism" for a long time...Those who promote this thinking...are trying to divide our country"; "You may now return to sucking donkey cocks for SATAN (aka George Soros)". The danger that I was taken to represent to "our society as Americans" was often stressed particularly in claims that identified me as one of the "woke destroyers of our society". The idea that I was simply one member of a far broader culture of corruption was an omnipresent theme; "you are part of a culture that is tearing this country apart with ideas...that have no relation to the world of the common man or woman". A type of American jingoism—or, perhaps more accurately, a type of White American Nationalism—was a prominent feature in these attacks:

> The only hope this planet is the white established...logic and drive of the Ol' U.S. of A.... America is being deflated and devalued due to a selfish, greedy group of Caucasians...and you are helping them... Mr. Hook, you're [sic] entire existence and development is based on standards and practices created by whites. It's incredibly hypocritical to bite the hand that has fed you from birth and given you everything you have and are.

My remarks were also attacked as anti-Christian, as anathema to Christian values and Catholicism in particular ("you represent speak for satan", "your comments ... re: white people ... are abhorrent", "your comments ... offend me ... as practicing Catholic"). For many of those who emailed me, I seemingly embodied "Absolute Psychotic Evil", "true evil", and I was as such deserving of appropriate forms of retribution ("I hope you burn in hell" was a much-repeated refrain). One email attacked me - erroneously - for quoting from the Bible and lamented that I made such comments "at a Catholic School...in a room filled with young adults", which of course, was untrue, as the talk was delivered online, in a purely individual capacity for a professional society.

What I am trying to stress here is not only the polarizing terms at work in such attacks, but also the attempt to position what I was thought to represent firmly in 'the enemy camp' as the absolute antithesis of conservative Christian American values (hence me being attacked as "Communist", "Marxist", etc. when there was no evidence for such claims). If this analysis holds, then what the attacks were most fundamentally about was far less the assumed content of my talk, than about how it might be utilized: as something to aggressively denounce as a means of affirming an opposed, and highly aggrieved, identity. In more straightforward terms: the messages played a role in consolidating—performing—an oppositional political identity.

The stance of aggrieved attack evinced by the emails often rehashed standard Trump-era conservative/Republican anti-liberal, anti-Democrat tropes, even though, it must be said, they were clearly voiced in a more febrile register, one adopting the ad hominem route of personalized attack. I was surprised by the fact that misrepresentations of my views were also seized upon by Republican politicians (and at least one Republican strategist). Larry Elder, for example, who, at the time running for the Governor of California, re-tweeted a post attacking my alleged statements. Re-postings by conservative pundits like Ann Coulter and a subsequent Fox News story (Colton, 2021) presumably had a similar political motivation: reinforcing a politics of grievance and resentment that linked together a variety of much maligned signifiers ("screaming liberals", Critical Race Theory, "Wokeness", Black Lives Matter, "DemocRats"). This, moreover, was part of a broader tactics of outrage, one which stoked the feeling that ordinary (white?) Americans were being persecuted, wronged by those, such as myself, holding extremist left-wing views.

There was—oddly perhaps—something vaguely consoling about this. While the attacks I received were obviously personalized, targeting, as they did, me and my alleged statements, these was nonetheless a sense in which this outrage, and these formulas of rebuke, long pre-dated my 'debuts' on Twitter and Fox News. It perhaps helps to note here that the attacks against me followed just a few months after a similar campaign of intimidation was launched against the psychoanalyst Donald Moss (as a result of his (2021) article 'On having whiteness'), and about 7 months after the attack on the US Capitol, which featured the participation of a series of hard-right groups (including: Proud Boys, Oath Keepers, Three Percenters, Patriot Movement, QAnon Movement, Neo-Confederates, Groypers, and others). I was at the same time a temporary focal point in a far broader program of rage and resentment, whilst remaining, in another way, incidental to it. Like the day's residue in Freud's *Interpretation of Dreams* (1900), what I was alleged to have said was a vehicle of transference, one which provided a means of expression for a wider set of grievances and hatreds. This was reflected in the comments offered by a colleague with experience in such online attacks: "Your life will be hell for a month, then your attackers will all move along to the next target, and you will be forgotten".

These observations point to the first general discursive theme to emerge from a reading of the emails. Their over-arching purpose was to consolidate an oppositional hard-right political identity—often, but not always of a generally White Nationalist sort—and, accordingly, to stoke a politics of grievance, and to do so by linking together a wide-ranging series of maligned signifiers associated with a progressive or leftist position. That the emails seemed so often to 'talk past me', to critique things that I hadn't said, and to target topics and identities beyond the obvious remit of both me and my talk ("Marxist parasites", "Bolshevik", "those who are "Vaxx compliant", "revenge politicians"," etc.) proved instructive here.[3] While what was being attacked was clearly something which had its coordinates in reality—an actual person, me—it is also a fantasy object. This fantasy object, moreover, was one which, in its various constituent parts, was the polar opposite of what the aggrieved subject identified with and held dear (i.e. it represents the inversion of their ideological ego-ideals). Hence the personifications of the sort: "YOU ARE EVERYTHING THAT IS WRONG TODAY'S SOCIETY". So, what was initially a rather vertiginous experience of being held to blame for a wide variety of stances, identities and values—some of which had little if any connection to my actual position—slowly started to make sense. In this sense, the scene of the attack in question was not merely a historical or discursive event, it was also a case of Freud's Other scene of fantasy.

Performative Offensiveness

A third general theme apparent within the emails was a type of *performative offensiveness*, by which I mean to refer to the demonstrative use of unreconstructed forms of racism/homophobia/anti-Semitism. The (5

September 2021) email cited at length above, for example, clearly resorts to a unreconstructed type of racism (use of the n-word, the wish that BLM advocates “deserve ... to be exterminated”). Disquieting as it was to receive such instances of racist hate-speech, the contents of such messages were not particularly surprising. Racist speech has long been connected to the tropes—and the enactments of—bodily violence, lynching, killing, and physical brutality. What accounts of large-scale campaigns of racist intimidation reveal (such as that of Yancy, 2018) is that while such language remains unacceptable within the broader public realm, the racist ideas continue to exert their force, and such sentiments are never that far from the surface even in more indirect, sophisticated (‘reconstructed’) or symbolic forms of racism.

In many instances the use of racist hate-speech was not linked to violent imagery, although there was an apparent relish in the use of forbidden or prohibited terms. The title of one representative email was: “professor, i am White. I hate [n-word] and [n-word]lovers like you”. There was a demonstrative quality to such messages; they showed me that, *yes*, this language can be used, and that *no*, despite the liberal hypocrisies of politically correct speech, the sender would speak, quite unrepentantly, in such terms, however much it might give offense. From a Lacanian standpoint, one would have to remark on the *jouissance* in question—that is, on the thrill of hate, the frisson of offensiveness (Hook, 2017, 2018, 2022)—incurred in those sending such messages and in enjoying the thought of their impact upon their recipient.

It was difficult at times to believe that all those attacking me were convinced that that I had indeed endorsed a program of white genocidal suicide. Perhaps some did; other seemed intent on believing it, motivated more by what they wished I’d said than by what I had said. Many “haters” presumably didn’t care; the opportunity to be scandalized and furious, and to go on attack, was simply enough. In other words, the rewards of enjoyment—of experiencing oneself as victimized, as persecuted, as righteously indignant—by far exceeded the agenda of rational assessment. Many of the messages seemed performative also in another sense. Not only did they perform *an act* in the terms outlined by speech act theory (an act of intimidation, disparagement, attack, etc.); they also indulged in the performance of a role, enacted a pretense of outrage. I frequently had the sense that many of my attackers were playing out an aggressive game of make-believe, in which willfully believing I’d said something was enough to justify attempts at doxing, getting me fired, hacking my email account, etc. This performative quality was also evident in the form of many of the messages I received. The voice messages often had a theatrical quality to them, as if the caller was doing their best to mime the formulas of horror movies in their attempt to be menacing ("Dr. Hook, the Jew professor", warned one caller, in a caricature of a creepy voice, "We're coming for you, believe it").

Many of those attacking me appeared to be doing so on a cynical basis; they were well aware that there was considerable doubt as to whether I had actually said what was being attributed to me. There was a discursive trace of this lack of conviction: even in some of the most vitriolic emails there were notable equivocations: "I understand that you were merely using another professor's theory and that these are not necessarily your thoughts or are they your thoughts as well?"; "Curious, did you really call for white people to commit suicide?"; "if this is true…"; "Did you actually suggest that white people should kill themselves?"; "this was a serious statement?", "comments in the media suggest you support the view that white people committing suicide would be an ethical act?".

We might again refer to Freud's (1900) ideas on dreams: when uncertainty or equivocation comes to the fore in the re-telling of a dream, the analyst can be sure that they have hit upon a weak point in the dreamer's defenses, that a suppressed thought is near the surface. Interestingly, Freud suggests that in such cases we take both sides of the equivocation seriously ("this is true", "this is not true"). Not only then does this lend support to what I have argued above (that equivocations are indicative of knowledge contrary to what is being suggested), it also points to the role of disavowal. A posture of implicit disavowal seemed apparent in a great many of the emails: "Yes, we know very well that there is considerable doubt as to whether Derek Hook called for the suicide of the white populace, but that doesn't matter, we are attacking him as if he did, nevertheless".

It is also helpful to adapt a Lacanian formulation here: many of my attackers received their own message back from me, albeit in in an inverted form (for Lacan (1988) "one receives one's own message from the other in an inverted form" (p. 51)). That is to say: their belief in a type of militant left-wing radicalism bent on destroying a conservative American way of life was proved correct by virtue of my alleged statements. Significantly also, many messages completely bypassed the content of my talk—as if to indicate that this was irrelevant—opting simply to highlight the fact of retribution: "LITTLE WHITE BOY GOING TO GET FIRED HAHAHAHAHAH", "WE ARE GOING TO DESTROY YOU ON SOCIAL MEDIA", and so on.

"'White' Is Not a Nation": Support from the Twitter-Sphere

Although I did not engage in any detail with the Twitter data, there is a brief thread of (anonymized) tweets posted between the 27 and 29 August 2021 that is worthwhile considering. It highlights some of the willful misreadings at play and also draws attention to how some of those who defended my position elaborated a version of my own position:

> Aug 25 2021:
>
> @MKE:
>
> Professor of Psychology at Duquesne University Derek Hook, defends the quote "white people should commit suicide as an ethical act" as an "opportunity" to "castrate whiteness".
>
> ...[...]...
>
> @Fa:
>
> He's not talking actual suicide. He's saying white south africans should integrate into the dominant culture and in the process give up their white identity.
>
> @JM
>
> That's still suicide. F that.
>
> ...[...]...
>
> @js:
>
> Again and again, systematically misinterpreting calls to end whiteness as a concept (eg like Germans ended Aryan identity) as calls to harm individual human beings who are white. Tenured professors have lost their jobs as targets of this deliberate misrepresentation. Enough.
>
> ...[...]...
>
> @em:
>
> Because the problem is [in mis-readings of Hook's position], people misinterpreting "white" as their nationality. "White" is not a nation. "White" is a collection of systemically racist, tribalist metaphors for power. We absolutely DO need to work on embracing culture/country/nation over just pallor.
>
> ...[...]...
>
> @km:
>
> No surprise. Provocative, violent rhetoric earned a visceral response. Metaphorical or not, targeting particular racial identities for demolition is functionally the same as the crudest race essentialism. Wholesale race abolitionism is the position consistent w/liberal ideals.
>
> @ja:

This is a bit confusing because wholesale race abolitionism does involve abolishing whiteness. I'm not quite grasping your logic of the last part of your argument here.

...[...]...

[This Tweet violated the Twitter rules]

@em:

Missing the entire point. No. What the original professor said, if you look at the context, is that whites in South Africa are a sociological model for whites in other countries--in that their perception of "whiteness" includes inflated self-superiority.

@er:

He was making the point--and this is the point you clearly missed--that as long as whites cling to their identity as INCLUDING systemic racism, then they cannot grow and change and become better.

@er:

IF YOU READ THE EXTRACT GIVEN, you will find the **EXACT CONTEXT** for [the statements Hook cites] is as follows: If white people are integrated fully into South African culture, instead of holding themselves apart as Other, then there will be no systemic racism....

@er:

...Because that inherent level of "whiteness" will be eliminated. Which is NOT cultural identity, it is NOT nationality, it is NOT race, it is purely and simply white fear.

...[...]...

@Xe:

so I can freely and openly call everywhere and everyone to murder white families, to kill white children, to rape white women, and if something happens, I just reply "no, you don't understand, it was a metaphor"

@em:

No. And that was not what was said. Again, read the original words in context. If you kill *anyone*, if you rape *anyone*, the societal hope overall is that you will be stopped, as you are a danger to that society. Shade of skin in that case does not matter.

@Xe:

He is not Bible or Quran to be interpreted as "a poetic metaphor and context" in violent text. If he means what you say, it would be "kill racism, supremacy", etc, as a trait. But he clearly tells about the whole identity, which is bad in its core, in every trait.

@er:

All right, yet again, I will do your work for you, since you'd rather be offended.... Your first mistake is misidentifying the target of your misplaced rage.

@Xe:

Thus the only way for a white to change is to kill himself or to erase his identity.

@er:

No, which is where your perceptions are skewed… I'm gonna try one more time then give up. I'm a white chick. I will always be a white chick. I don't see a reason I can--or should--stop living just because I'm white. I DO feel I'm a part of a burdensomely racist system.

@er:

So it is MY RESPONSIBILITY as a white adult to realize I have privilege, to use that to foster the causes of other humans who are not given my perceived advantages due to said systemic racism, and to stomp out racist beliefs in myself.

This was an instructive set of exchanges; it shows that what I was arguing was, while provocative, not hopelessly obscure, or even particularly difficult to grasp. From the outset of the attacks, I felt that it was important to dismiss the all-too easy (if understandable) defensive reaction: Those who are attacking you are ignorant. Despite the obvious prejudice embodied in such a defense, it overlooked what I took to be crucial: anyone who took the time to consider my position could appreciate the gist of my argument. Ignorance was not the issue. There was evidence that those attacking me grasped not only the non-literal dimension of my argument but also the hypothetical nature of the ethical dilemma. For example: "I understand that you were dealing with what if's", "If yours was a thought experiment it is a dangerous one for people like me"; "Whether you meant spiritually white suicide to somehow give equity to…or literal committing suicide matters little".

Supportive commentators usefully distinguished between literal suicide, on the one hand, and ideas pertaining to the relinquishing of structural privilege and the associated condition of "inflated self-superiority", on the other. Despite this qualification, one participant nonetheless concluded: "That's still suicide". Similarly instructive was the distinction offered between 'whiteness' as a concept—an inherently discriminatory signifier, a marker of privilege/superiority (like the notion of the Aryan race, as one participant noted), on the one hand, and "individual human beings who are white", on the other. Another revealing moment occurred here. In response to the charge levelled at me of "Wholesale race abolition", a defender noted, that abolition of whiteness *as a concept*, as structure of privilege, or, to extend the point, as narcissistic signifier of superiority, was precisely the point, even though, to cite a further defender, white individuals would continue to exist ("I'm a white chick. I always will be a white chick").

A few personal reflections seem justified here. The above Twitter exchange helped alleviate the disorientation effect of the attacks. A handful of politically offensive messages, while unpleasant, can be dismissed as extreme, unrepresentative. To be subjected to hundreds of affronted emails and phone messages, on the other hand, starts, even if only incrementally, to shift your sense of what an average, median or centrist political might be. In Lacanian terms: one loses a sense of where the big Other might be expected to stand in respect of such issues. I started to believe that the general social consensus on such issues was far more to the right of the political spectrum than I had previously assumed. Hard-right White nationalist views were being repeatedly expressed as standard beliefs, as accepted norms of American society, and in such a way that those expressing such views felt in no way compromised by sharing them. These were defensible views, views that would utlimately be vindicated—such was the message being conveyed.

This disorientation effect involved a degree of paranoid thinking (a situation not helped by the fact that at least one threatening phone message came from a number from within my own university). I began to wonder to what extent the views expressed in the attacking messages were shared by many of my associates and peers. When I was in public spaces—commuting to work, doing grocery shopping, being amongst other parents at school functions, etc.—I started to wonder: which of you might have fired off an incensed email or taken to Twitter to threaten or castigate me?

There was another insidious effect related to the cumulative effect of the attacks. I have already noted the unintentional humor of some of the messages. This laughable element, I told myself, made it alright, the mindless repetition of certain phrases ("You go first", etc.) would eventually lead to a degree of desensitization. It helped in this respect that so many of the messages were formulaic in nature ("I know where you live…"). Being able scroll through pages and pages of vulgar and threatening communications, and be OK with it, was, so I thought, a sign of resilience. I consoled myself with the thought that for many high-profile figures this is simply a fact of life. Perhaps, I thought, this becomes routine. And then, despite these self-consoling thoughts, there would be one phone message or emailed image that would deviate from the template and touch a nerve.

Perverse Intimidations

Let us return to a more analytical stance and take up question related to the topic of the offensiveness of the emails: what were attackers *attempting to do with their offensiveness*? The demonstrative offensiveness of the emails noted above was also apparent in the amount homophobia on display. I was initially surprised by this, given that issues of sexuality or sexual orientation do not feature at all in my original analysis of white anxiety. Comments such as "what does a male cock taste like?", "I'm going to visit you on campus ... You don't want to get the police involved, Keep sucking Muslim [expletive] until I arrive", "lefty pathetic faggot POS", and "You cocksucking ... maggot" and "I bet you cry at night while being fucked in your ass!", "eat dicks" were very frequent. One email, copied into half a dozen colleagues at Duquesne University read as follows:

> *Go to hell Hook*. You do NOT think for me... The exact same b shit a few lesbian SW [Social Work] Prof's tried to indoctrinate us with, messages like: you are all homosexuals that are out of touch with your sexuality...you really do represent...satan.

Remarks pertaining to either my sexual humiliation ("Does your husbands boyfriend realize how much of a cuck you are?") or my apparently evident perversity were commonplace (i.e. "next time you do your autoerotic asphyxiation masturbation rituals...just leave the belt around your neck"; "you should stay away from children; you look like a pedophile", "I hope you chomo [slang for child molester] choke on a HUGE bag of dicks"). There was also a series of grotesque racist rape fantasies sketched out, in which I—or my family as a whole—were subjected to various forms of attack ("I hope you get raped to death by a pack of feral [racist expletive] ..."). These were invariably racist and were often mixed with images of sexual abjection and bestiality.

It was significant that many attacks mentioned my family. This, of course, is a basic—and typically effective—intimidation tactic. One of the most frightening aspects of the hate campaign was that one of my attackers zoomed in to the background of the room in which I had delivered my original lecture, enlarging several times over pictures of my children, and then posting them alongside a thread of threatening tweets. The implication of such messages was that my family was a stain to the white bloodline ("you ... [should be] cancelled along with your entire family lineage", "you can … help your white evil BS by assuring America you will not contribute to the white gene pool in future"; "I propose [he] … removes himself from the planet and from the genepool"; "I'll be … waiting for [the] cleansing from … whiteness that you so deserve". I was also advised to "trade in your wife and children … to the first non-White person you meet today"). Not only was all of this linked to the antisemitic comments in many of the attacks (which I turn to shortly), it also resonated with racist notions of racial impurity, indeed, with colonial racism's preoccupation with miscegenation.

An idea from a Lacanian conceptualization of perversion proved useful as a way of positioning in this respect. If such messages were deliberately designed to offend me, to cause intense negativity of affect, if, in other words, they acted, in Lacanian terms, precisely as perverse provocations (Hook, 2022; Swales, 2012), then it was important to bear this agenda in mind and, accordingly, to not take the bait, avoid succumbing to the outraged reaction that the emails hoped to elicit. While there were obvious limits to how much I could treat the material in a detached way—as research data, as so obviously performed in order to elicit disturbing affect—I found that this insight did often help ground me. I did not of course, respond to any of the messages I received, so such an attitude of detachment would have been lost on my attackers, but it proved helpful as both a self-protective measure and as a methodological/analytical stance in respect of exploring the material.

Accusations/Denials/Expressions of Racism

Many emails alleged that I was racist: "Your ideas are racist and just as bad as the KKK, The Nazi's et al."; "encouraging people to commit suicide because of there skin colour is just another form of nazism"; "very racist … could be seen … as a call to hurt or kill white people". These claims were invariably premised on an *assumption of equivalence* regards the social structures pertaining to whiteness and Blackness. Such an assumption of course overlooks both the privileges that have typically accrued to white populations and the historical legacies of racism within countries such as South Africa and the United States. The denial of such social asymmetries was a reoccurring theme, linked to the perceived injustice expressed in many of the emails: "There is NO systemic racism. Period"; "What's next? Reparations? Again, punish those who never trespassed to aggrieve those who never suffered. Brilliant".

Some attacks of this sort sounded more reasonable than others: "if this would be inappropriate to apply to ALL races, it is inappropriate for one particular race"; "How is that not racism to pass judgement on an entire race?"; "Do you think hate of any race of people is … moral?" The reasoning in attacks of this sort would often replace the signifier 'white' with 'black', such that any attacks on whiteness *as structure of privilege* could be made to look blatantly racist when addressed toward Black people. For example: "Do you…teach that to prevent black supremacy, blacks should kill themselves?"; "[what] if you were to use a lecture from a white professor … presenting a radical theory about…ending blackness/black culture … [?]". Such a strategy—effectively a denial of structural racism assuming the guise of anti-racism—is, of course, nothing new. It parallels the riposte that "White lives matter", and echoes contemporary attempts to downplay, sideline, or effectively silence the roles that slavery and institutionalized racism have played in the history of the United States.

One reason that the 'level playing field' argument featured so frequently was that it provided a basis for the claim that whites are being unfairly persecuted and victimized: "[this] demonization of white culture seems indistinguishable from the early days of Nazi Germany…[it is] potentially lethal"; "Your bigotry is disgraceful…you spew hatred against white people"; "Whites are the only group of people it is apparently acceptable to advocate self-harm for in the academic context"; "you [are] not in the business of education but the business of white revenge [i.e. revenge on whites]". The insistence on whites as victims was often accompanied by the claim that the real issue was the anti-white racism of Blacks: "racism today…has been and continues to be a major phenomenon in among the Black population … [it] predominates [there] more than in the White community". Many anecdotal examples were forthcoming: "I remember our station wagon being surrounded… by a gang of black teenagers at 4 yrs old and my dad telling my brothers and I to lock the doors…as the group surrounded us and beat on the vehicle".

The motif of the violent Black gang was often invoked, sometimes in the form of an aggressive wish-fulfilment ("[You will be] obducted by a group of African American, BLM hoodlums"). A different example comes from a lengthy essay I received listing a litany of crimes perpetrated by Blacks against whites:

> [R]acial tensions... [are] exacerbated by such groups as "Black Lives Matters" and "The Knockout" craze perpetrated by gangs of young Black men/boys against unsuspecting innocent White People... [These gangs] converge on shopping malls attacking undeserving White shoppers and of course taking/stealing/shoplifting all the merchandise they can carry. Let us not forget "Rap Music", and videos calling White People condescending names: honkies, rednecks, crackers, peckerwoods.

I was presented with statistics ostensibly proving that people of color were over-represented amongst violent criminal offenders, just as whites were over-represented as victims: "87% of all violent crimes are committed by the nonwhites per FBI and USDOJ data and studies ... [if that] 87% would commit suicide, it would be for the betterment of the collective as related to our society's safety". Another example of such an argumentative attempt to prove the superiority of whites involved the appeal—in a surprisingly number of the emails—to IQ scores. One email asked: "Why would Gods chosen and the savior of all other inferior, low IQ races kill themselves?" Another cited a (2010) article by Lynn & Meisenberg, 'The average IQ of Sub-Saharan Africans' to justify their conclusions:

> [T]he average IQ of sub-Saharan Africans is about 80... The international studies of mathematics, science, and reading give a sub-Saharan African IQ of 66....data sets can be averaged to give an IQ of 68 as the best reading of the IQ in sub-Saharan Africa.

If, as a Lacanian perspective suggests, any inter-subjective communication is always also an intra-subjective communication, one could ask of such oft-repeated "proofs" of white moral/intellectual superiority: "Just who are you trying to convince?"

Whereas some attackers adopted the rhetorical strategy of asserting that all races should be viewed equally—so as to argue that any critique of whiteness was effectively racist - others simply affirmed that whites are exceptional and deserving of gratitude from all other racial groups:

> Do you realize that under British rule the population of South Africa increased dramatically, life expectancy doubled, as vaccines and modern medicine were introduced? Most children survived rather than died. Be honest and write about how black and brown people throughout much of the world owe literally everything to their former colonizers. Everything. They should express gratitude.

Such a defense of the merits of colonial rule occurred repeatedly. Similarly, many emails extolled the virtues of white European civilization:

> Don't you realize the Caucasian race and it's reasoning is the only hope for this planet? There is so much talk about White Nationalists these days. Don't you realize we're all White Nationalists? You, me, Oprah Winfrey, Barack Obama, Jennifer Lopez, Jackie Chan. We all live in a civilization based on the collective history, experience and struggle of humans descended from Western and Northern Europeans influenced by the Indo European civilizations of Greece and Rome .... If you are capable of being honest with yourself, you'll admit, maybe reluctantly, that there isn't a successful Black government on the face of the Earth. Not a one....

An important sidenote here concerns how whiteness was qualified and described in these emails. Interestingly, the above email, after praising the cultural achievements of Caucasians, goes on to specify that Europeans, while technically part of the same group,

> are cultural and social Neanderthals compared to us...Americans in the New World... We Americans are the best version of this branch of the human family.

The narcissistic form of white identification on display is here unabashedly American. This remark was representative of a reoccuring theme in the emails. It confirmed the importance for me of speaking about White Nationalism rather than merely about 'whiteness' in describing the position of outrage and opposition that my attackers were writing from. This is not of course to say that they would necessarily identify with this term—which of course has negative connotations—although it is an accurate way of describing the ideological standpoint of the majority of attacking messages that I received.

Race-Traitor as Ideological Dilemma

The following email reiterates many of the themes we have discussed, offering, in addition, a speculative psychological diagnosis to account for my alleged remarks and a few further notes exemplifying characteristics of 'whiteness':

> [Hook's comments] appears to me to be an intellectually sublimated form of self-hatred, a familiar species of institutionally-inculcated mental illness

> prevalent among "woke" academics... So Hook's emphasis is on cutting "whiteness" (work ethic, punctuality, correct grammar and spelling, mathematical skills, emphasis on individual accountability, individual justice and individual rights, and so on).... Clearly it is the mass of "whites" in the US (read: European Americans) who are the target of this hybrid class warfare inflicted on them by virtue signaling white political elites.

Aside from the series of disqualifying remarks aimed at myself (self-hatred, institutionally induced mental illness, "woke-ness", being a virtue-signaling member of the political elite), what seems most interesting here is the list of characteristics of "whiteness". Virtue signaling seems, in fact, an apt phrase to describe part of what is going on here: "whiteness" is couched in terms of moral exemplarity ("accountability, justice, individual rights"). "Whiteness" moreover is harmless; it does not reside in power-relations or privilege but is evinced rather in those small but important virtues ("work ethic, punctuality...mathematical skills") which keep society running. The reiteration of these attributes also, of course, codes for their opposites; the implication being that those who are not white lack such qualities. The strategy of re-framing whiteness such that it is not a question of structural privilege but rather a collection of benevolent, virtuous cultural traits shared by white people, is likewise apparent in the following:

> I hope to hear that you get removed from the college and placed in a mental healthcare facility. Then you'll learn being white is so magical and wonderful. White people believe in nice community's and values. White people are great people and without white people, you never would have become a professor. So, your welcome.

Leaving aside the evident contradiction at hand—that despite apparently being "wonderful" and "great", many white people were quite capable of some pretty horrendous intimidation tactics—it is worth stressing again the idea that whiteness is owed something, that those who are not white (or those who critique it) remain fundamentally indebted to it.

What many of the above-cited extracts point to is an ideological dilemma—a paradox of sorts—that many of my attackers needed to try and explain: how was it that I, a white person, would go about critiquing whiteness? This might not seem at first glance an intractable dilemma. The again, if we consider the assumptions of race essentialism, which, of course, underlie so much racist thinking, then, we understand that however morally problematic and corrupt the figure of Derek Hook might be, he, as white, cannot summarily be rejected from the category of whiteness. One ready-to-hand response to this dilemma was the charge that I was "nothing more than a race traitor". We have already been introduced to two further related responses: the contention, firstly, that I suffered from a type of self-hatred ("your intense public self-loathing", "you have so much self-hatred for your own race", etc.), and, secondly, that I suffered from some or other sort of institutional-indoctrination and/or mental illness ("You should seek help… for your mental disorders"). An even more frequently noted rebuke—which I discuss below —was the attack of hypocrisy. In each of these discursive moves (allegations of being a race traitor, of pathology, of hypocrisy), I remained within the fold of whiteness. True enough, there were attempts to separate me from Americanness ("you fucking limey pussy"; "I see you live abroad (not US)"; "YOU WILL NOW HAVE…TO GO BACK HOME PERMANENTLY"), but it was not possible within the confines of essentialist discourses of race, to 'excommunicate' me from whiteness, with one very significant exception, to which we now turn.

Antisemitism

While I could have anticipated much of the racism contained within the barrage of hate mail I received, I was blindsided by the degree of the antisemitism contained in the attacks. Take for example the following:

> You do realize that white people have literally created everything? And that white people have been the most enslaved race of all time? ... I'm just gonna go out on a limb here and guess your jewish…I am certain I am right on this…there is truth in your speech [it is that] jews…and their jealousy to be…the real chosen race…the white race have yet again shown that everything a jew does or says is so massively inflated to make them look better…the truth of their real goal [is]…destroying white people… But I'm here to tell you money changer…you are a mut who has tried to claim you pure breedness… Good day Mr Jewish Professor cause I know you probably trying to take some Palestinians house for your own and saying God gave it you… Did you get your degree at Aushwitchs University? Double majors and 6 million lies?

A similar email arrived later the same day:

> **Subject: [External] The White Race Will Not Perish**
> You're a loxist Jew aren't you. The spirit of Hitler lives in many Whites and you kikes are going to pay for your loxism. Keep pushing us you fucking jew and you will be sorry

The first of these emails interweaves a series of antisemitic stereotypes and slurs; both emails entail disturbing references to the Holocaust, which the first email implicitly denies, even as the second draws on the "The spirit of Hitler" in its attempts at intimidation. (Loxism, incidentally, is an antisemitic term, which refers to the alleged irrational hatred of white Europeans by Jewish peoples).

My colleague Stephen Frosh (forthcoming) has offered incisive commentary on the role of antisemitism in these attacks, so I will limit my comments here to just a few observations that build on the analysis offered above. Firstly, as any student of antisemitism will know, whenever anti-Black racism is present—or, we might add, any aggressive defense of 'Whiteness' is on display—then anti-Semitism is invariably also present. There is, as such, an important corollary to Frantz Fanon's memorable remark according to which the Black man or woman, upon hearing an antisemitic remark, should be aware that this prejudice pertains to them also ("When you hear someone insulting the Jews, pay attention; he is talking about you" (2008, p. 101)). To adapt Fanon: "When you hear someone derogating Black people, pay attention; they are derogating Jews also".

Secondly, antisemitism appeared, at least in part, to offer a solution of sorts to the ideological dilemma noted above: how to situate someone who is both undeniably (visually) white, yet who nevertheless embodies a potent *internal* threat to whiteness? It is significant that the equivocations—and perverse disavowals—discussed earlier were particularly pronounced in respect of the question of whether or not I was Jewish. Both the above cited emails pose this question before going on to conclude that I was in fact Jewish. This was not an isolated trend. Consider the following: "do I have it wrong and you're (((Jewish))) and therefore not White? You look white or are you a jewish white" and "You look white or are you a jewish white, which is apparently exempt". Interestingly, the very suspension of certainty in this respect, the guessing of whether or not I ("Dr Hooknose", "Rabbi Hook") was Jewish speaks to one of the key tropes of anti-Semitism—the nervously uncategorizable status of the Jew (Strosberg, 2023).

The need to position me in relation to whiteness adhered to a certain logic, which took the following form. You are in some ways (visually) white, but you can't be fully white—or fully *American white*—because: (a) you are in some respects non-American, an immigrant, a foreigner; (b) you are actually only a pathological or deviant ("self-loathing", "self-hating") white, an irremediable hypocrite, a "race traitor"; (c) you are Jewish and as such have never been anything more than an ambiguous or provisional inclusion in whiteness.

Aggressive Cordiality

It is worth noting that the two antisemitic emails cited above were signed off in the sender's name (i.e., not sent in a disguised form or from an anonymized address). This was a further aspect of the attacks that I was taken aback by. Barring a few exceptions, the majority of emails that I received—including many of the most extreme, expletive-filled and racist/anti-Semitic examples—were accompanied by the sender's name and email address (and included in some instances additional identifying information, telephone numbers, residential addresses, etc.). While I was obviously not able to check this information in every case, it certainly appeared legitimate. Ultimately what was most significant in this respect was not whether the contact information actually checked out, but what the attackers conveyed to me by the gesture of including it, namely: we are unafraid to identify ourselves; we do not fear recrimination. As one of my attackers put it: "And yes this is my real name I'm not afraid". Identifying themselves was part of the point.

The prevalence of identity markers in the emails was notable. To give a few examples: "I am conservative, a Texas rancher, 64 years old"; "I also have a PhD"; "I am a white guy, married to a Black professional lady"; "I am a former police officer and a veteran of the US Army"; "a practicing Catholic", "A concerned Christian"; "Afghanistan Combat Veteran"; "I am White, Southern, male (not Christian, but close enough), and am a raving maniacal Trump voter". Some of the emails solicited a response. While obviously this was in many cases insincere, merely a rhetorical or threatening gesture ("May I ask Sir------ are you a communist?....I would like a clear response on this"; "I invite you to my house... ...Bring friends...Call for directions to the house"), in others it was apparently sincere ("Having lived in South Africa...you will understand my interest in your comments... Please respond when you get the opportunity"). An unexpected cordiality was sometimes evident. In addition to offering overtures to dialogue or further interaction ("I would like to say I am available to present, lecture, defend, debate"; "I welcome to any feedback"), some messages sought to offer advice: "I suggest henceforth you balance your thesis on racial matters"; "Read Matthew 22:37, that's the ticket"; "I beg you to dig deeper into history". Disingenuous or not, such message called for a response; they implied the structure of a dialogue.

While a great many unpleasant things were wished upon me, and many implied threats were expressed, I did not receive a direct, unequivocal death-threat, at not least via email (I routinely deleted telephone messages from unknown numbers without listening to them; such threats would have been far more likely in this anonymized form). This no doubt sets me apart from colleagues who have been subjected to similar campaigns of intimidation, and who most certainly have received explicit threats of this sort. There are many possible reasons for such hesitancy on the part of my attackers. One pragmatic consideration is that a concrete death-threat is 'actionable', it provides the basis to open a police investigation which can create complications for the sender of the message. Yet this was surely not the only factor at play. The aggressive cordiality of the emails was, I think, a result of the fact that as a white person—admittedly of a highly problematic sort—I might still be rescued, retrieved from the "woke indoctrination" to which I had succumbed. After all, despite being a "race traitor" I was still white, and from the standpoint of essentialist race/racist thinking (as already noted), once white always white (except, of course in the case of Jewishness, where whiteness, so it seems, is only ever provisional).

This perhaps accounts for the many personal anecdotes shared with me by whites about their alleged experiences of Black anti-white racism, just as it explains attempts to show me the error of my ways—via crime statistics, pseudo-scientific studies, historical evidence, etc.—and thereby persuade me to come around to their way of thinking. The form of the emails was significant in this respect. Whereas around half were, admittedly, simply derogatory "fuck you" messages which aimed only to insult or intimidate without any further communicative intent, approximately a third of the emails did take on a more dialogical form. A potential overture to a further dialogue was on offer. One email reassured me: "Should you come to your senses, this groups of Caucasians will welcome you back into the fold". Now while, to be sure, only a very small portion of emails offered this option—a kind of olive branch of whiteness—it seems abundantly clear that had I not been white, such overtures to dialogue would have been less present, just as there would have been less tentativeness in respect of the threats issued.

Whiteness at the Abyss

By way of conclusion, let me change tack and briefly reflect on some reasonable critical comments contained within the emails. This may sound a little odd, given the overwhelmingly aggressive and offensive nature of the messaging as foregrounded above. Nevertheless, there were a small minority of emails that were, I think, sent in good faith, by people with legitimate concerns, who felt it necessary to voice their position to me, often with sincere requests for further discussion or clarification. Bearing this in mind it seems important also to consider how my own enunciative position—surely an important factor for any psychoanalytically oriented approach—might be brought into question and reflected upon. As an aside, we might note this as a limitation of how psychoanalysis is sometimes utilized as a form of social critique: a formidable array of psychanalytic concepts can be drawn upon so as to analyze or deconstruct that which we are critical of, without necessarily bearing in mind how our own position of critical exception might also be in need of analysis.

As theorists of the psychic dimension of political life, we often prove adept at bringing the theoretical apparatus of psychoanalysis to bear as a means of critique, without adequately taking our positions of enunciation into account.

A first criticism concerned the apparent irresponsibility of the style of my presentation and the extremity of the language used. I was chided for making such polemical arguments, and for adopting an overly provocative rhetorical style, in a public forum. While I have taken this criticism to heart, I will add that the style of my presentation was not unconsidered. It was appropriate for the professional psychoanalytic group for whom it was intended—a group which had, after all, gathered precisely to consider the topic of deconstructing whiteness. One retort to this would be: in today's always-potentially online world remarks of this sort are never going to be contained within the bounds of a scholarly/professional setting. The implications of this situation and of the fact that such online intimidation strategies can be enforced against academics at any time, is deserving of a fuller discussion than I can offer here. Suffice to say: these new social media circumstances are not going away anytime soon. The above account might be read as a cautionary tale—one which begs multiple questions, to be sure, in respect of critical pedagogy, the risks of making of provocative arguments, etc. And yet it might also be taken as an invitation to think strategically, creatively, about what new possibilities for critique, social engagement and solidarity might now be possible.

A second and perhaps more substantive criticism, focused on the apparent hypocrisy of my position. This was frequently highlighted by my attackers. Regards such claims, I am of two minds. I would suggest, as a first response, that I was more sympathetic to, 'whiteness'—whiteness understood here as a set of racial/historical/cultural identifications—than many of my attackers realized. I argued that "the prospective end of an ego…of a set of identifications … [and] the potentiality of anxiety [this involves]…entails the prospect of radical transformation" (2020b, p. 108). Moreover: "to speak of the end of an ego … [in this case, the end of identifications of whiteness] is not to simply to speak of death, but of an event in which something new may emerge" (2020b, p. 109). Transformation here, in other words, is not tantamount to eradication or extinction. While the prospect of radical change to a given set of (imaginary/symbolic) identifications may certainly feel like an end - may, indeed, be experienced as an instance of castration -it can in fact be the first step in a psychical process that involves making identifications of a different sort. Or, to make the point in Lacanian terms: to traverse a fantasy—that is, to facilitate a re-orientation in respect of a structuring fundamental fantasy (Lacan, 1981)—involves the prospect of a crossing over, a relocation, a possible *working through*, as opposed to a project of pure and simple erradication.

True, these remarks are unlikely to assuage the concerns of those who are determined to insist that 'whiteness'—understood as a nation of *white American people* rather than *a structural form of cultural privilege*—is being threatened with persecution and erasure. From such a standpoint, whiteness remains a master-signifier of fantasmatic identity that must remain beyond the level of scrutiny. Incidentally, I was reminded, in the aftermath of the attacks, of a comment by the Žižek scholar, Tony Myers, who offered a warning in relation to any critical apprehension of another's fantasy:

> [E]ach individual's fantasy is the support of his or her being ... it is extremely precious and therefor sensitive to the encroachment of others ... [fantasy] is ... the tender nerve or raw ganglia of the subject's psyche ... it is liable to cause grave distress if we probe it with insufficient care. (Myers, 2003, p. 103)

I am, surely, guilty in respect of such an encroachment; an encroachment for which I paid the price. Contrary however to the above standpoint (whiteness as beyond scrutiny), I do, obviously, feel that the whiteness can be called into scrutiny, both at the psychic level (of narcissistic identification/fantasy) and at that of structural privilege.

A further aside seems warranted here. It is perhaps telling that in the above lines I differentiate between forms of whiteness (psychical as opposed to socio-structural). One of my attackers made a relevant point, which, I would suggest, is worthwhile bearing in mind in respect critiques of whiteness more generally: "[as] his vague term "whiteness" goes without specific definition, a listener would have to assume Asst. Prof. Hook means "white people" as "whiteness" but his phraseology is structured in a way where the definition is malleable depending on the argument". Although I would want to stress that I did add a clear definition of whiteness as "white privilege ... as structure of domination" (see the previous chapter, but also: Hook, 2020b, p. 92), it is true that such a structure has—unavoidably perhaps—psychical correlates and that in utilizing the term critically there is a constant possibility of slipping between two interrelated but conceptually distinct terms of reference. This issue has been addressed in the literature via distinctions between whiteness (as form of structural privilege) and 'whiteliness' (a type of dispositionality enacted by those who have benefitted from white privilege). Nevertheless, I will remain vigilant in respect of reiterating and maintaining this distinction in subsequent work.

While discussing the importance of definitional clarity in critiques of whiteness, I should note a further point impressed upon me by the experience of the attacks, and more specifically, by the antisemitism contained in the attacks. There is often an assumption, in more totalizing critical references to whiteness, that intersectional differentiations within this group do not particularly matter. As the foregoing analysis shows, this is too much of an assumption to make. As Strosberg (2023) puts it: "The idea of universal inclusion into privilege and Whiteness also contributes to contemporary forms of antisemitism which exclude Jewish particularity, culture [and] diversity ... from discussion" (p. 52).

All of the above being said, I will say that the many accusations of hypocrisy did touch a nerve. I am forced to concede: to critique white structural privilege from a position of white structural privilege is hypocritical. (This, I should note, differs from the type of hypocrisy that I was far more frequently accused of, namely, that of being a white person critiquing whiteness, i.e. essentially a "race traitor", which is a charge that I find both less than necessarily hypocritical and less bothersome). Why do I make this concession? Well, as the level of anxiety ratcheted up as the attack campaign against me grew and grew, my partner asked: "What are you most anxious about in all of this?" This was a suitably psychoanalytic question because what it was really asking was: "What is the *other* anxiety lying behind the anxieties that you are willing to admit to?" As the answers accumulated—the possibility of an actual attack, the risk to the security of my children, the prospective loss of my job, financial insecurity, etc.—I inched closer to an irrational fear that I hadn't quite admitted to myself. If enough people, with enough political power clout had been angered by me, then my US visa and my recently issued green card, could be rescinded, and my family would be forced to leave the country. This would mean that we could lose the middle-class existence, the comfortable suburban way of life, that we had become so used to. In other words, what I was afraid of losing, was, in large part, privilege itself.

One might ask what the Lacanian dimension was to this situation. Well, in the introductory chapter, I briefly cited my own description of Lacan's (1992) notion of subjective destitution:

> Subjective destitution connotes the state ... whereby one has surrendered one's agalma ... the secret treasure of 'that in me more than me' ... Lacan's [concept of] *object a*, the object cause of desire, or, differently put, that *je ne sais* quoi property which defines what is most loveable in me. To surrender this object effectively 'desubjectivizes' the subject. It means not only to have deflated one's narcissistic fantasies, but to have foregone...[the] imagined transcendence of what is most base about oneself, to accept one's status as excremental remainder. (Hook, 2011b, p. 502)

I would be reticent to claim that I had undergone something quite so unrelenting and fraught as what Lacan (1992) apparently had in mind with this concept (i.e. a situation where all of a subject's imaginary attachments are potentially severed or radically re-evaluated). Yet the above description has a resonance in that it indicates a point of imagined transcendence. I will say that if my point of "imagined transcendence", that is, my *object a*, had something to do with somehow implicitly extricating myself from whiteness (by virtue of mounting a critical exploration/analysis of whiteness), then this narcissistic fantasy most certainly did undergo a re-alignment.

Whether the foregoing reflections invalidate my study of white anxiety, or my attempted exploration of whiteness at the abyss, well, this is something that remains for the reader to decide, although I would like to hope that the relevance of a critical argument—or an ethical dilemma—is not wholly contingent on the person who delivers it. And so, although in this respect the jury is still out, there is something of which we can be sure. The ethical dilemma involved in considering the end of white privilege ceased to be merely intellectual issue for me. Even if only for a short period of time, and in a limited and ultimately sheltered way, this dilemma, and the choice it entailed, rebounded on me in the form of an experience of vulnerability and anxiety from which I learnt a great deal.

Notes

1. A colleague who helped me translate an email that I received from Germany noted that the message was weirdly worded, probably as "a loophole way to avoid a law which makes insulting or threatening people illegal/punishable by fines or light jail terms". The senders of some of the antisemitic material I received certainly would be criminal liable—in terms of laws against hate speech, against holocaust denialism—if these messages had been sent from Germany.
2. Without belaboring the obvious, there is simply not the same vocabulary of hate available to attack a white, straight, CIS-gender, non-religious man such as myself as compared to what is available to derogate persons of color, women, the LGBQT folks, and those of faiths that appear to be outside the mainstream of conservative American values.
3. Within the terms of the psychoanalytic discourse theory described by Ernesto Laclau (2007) and Slavoj Žižek (1989), we could loosely conceptualize this as the maintenance and expansion of a hegemonic—indeed, populist—discourse. Such a hegemonic discourse becomes operative when it achieves the 'buy-in of' diverse and otherwise disparate communities of interest whose libidinal passions come to be united via the joint articulation or 'quilting function' of a series of oft-reiterated and much-maligned signifiers.

References

Colton, E. (2021). *Pennsylvania professor teacher White people committing suicide can be an 'ethical' act*, 2 September. Retrieved from https://www.foxnews.com/us/professor-white-people-committing-suicide-ethical-act

DiAngelo, R. (2018). *White Fragility*. Beacon Press.

Fanon, F. (2008). *Black Skin, White Masks*. Grove Press.

Freud, S. (1900/1955). The Interpretation of Dreams. *Standard Edition* 4–5 (pp. 1–751). Hogarth Press.

Frosh, S. (forthcoming). On academic freedom, provisional whiteness and Antisemitism. *Psychoanalysis, Culture & Society*.

Hook, D. (2011b). White privilege, psychoanalytic ethics and the limitations of political silence. *South African Journal of Philosophy 30*(3), 495–502.

Hook, D. (2017). What is 'enjoyment as a political factor'? *Political Psychology, 38*(4), 605–620.

Hook, D. (2018). Racism and jouissance: Evaluating the 'racism as (the theft of) enjoyment' hypothesis. *Psychoanalysis, Culture and Society, 23*(3), 244–266.

Hook, D. (2020a). White anxiety in (post)apartheid South Africa. *Psychoanalysis, Culture and Society, 25*, 612–631.

Hook, D. (2020b). 'The white centreline vanishes': Fragility and anxiety in the elusive metropolis. In N. Falkof & C. van Staden (Eds.), *Anxious Joburg: The Lives of a Global South City*. Wits University Press.

Hook, D. (2022). Perverse act, gaze and structure. *Psychoanalytic Practice, 30*(1), 10–38.

Lacan, J. (1981). In J-A. Miller (Ed.), *The Seminar of Jacques Lacan: Book XI: The Four Fundamental Concepts of Psychoanalysis* (A. Sheridan, Trans.). Norton.

Lacan, J. (1988). In J-A. Miller (Ed.), *The Seminar of Jacques Lacan: Book II: The Ego in Freud's Theory and in the Technique of Psychoanalysis* (S. Tomaselli, Trans.). Norton.

Lacan, J. (1992). In J-A. Miller (Ed.), *The Seminar of Jacques Lacan: Book VII: The Ethics of Psychoanalysis* (D. Porter, Trans.). Norton.

Laclau, E. (2007). *Emancipations*. Verso.

Lynn, R., & Meisenberg, G. (2010). The average IQ of sub-Saharan Africans: Comments on Wicherts, Dolan, and van der Maas. *Intelligence, 38*(1), 21–29.

Moss, D. (2021). On having Whiteness. *Journal of the American Psychoanalytical Association, 69*(2), 355–371.

Myers, T. (2003). *Slavoj Žižek*. Routledge.

Strosberg, B. (2023). *Negative Psychology of Anti-Semitism: Fear of the Uncategorizable*. Unpublished PhD Dissertation, Duquesne University, Pittsburgh.

Swales, S. (2012). *Perversion*. Routledge.

Yancy, G. (2018). *Backlash: What Happens When We Talk Honestly About Racism in America*. Rowman & Littlefield.

Zeavin, H. (2022). Unfree association: Parasitic whiteness and off the couch. *N+1*, 42, Spring. Retrieved from https://www.nplusonemag.com/issue-42/essays/unfree-associations/

Žižek, S. (1989). *The Sublime Object of Ideology*. Verso.

Afterword

Donald Moss

Whiteness, when it expresses itself as white supremacy, seems to work as though it were a single organism, a lumbering beast astride this world of ours. The beast has a voice, of course, one clear voice. While unencumbered, that voice swaggers—commanding, wicked and tyrannical. The beast roams, the entire planet serving as its niche. It assumes itself an apex predator confident of its position beyond the reach of threat. Whiteness as predator can afford the quiet sonorities of an absolute ruler. It can marshal the language of reason, as though it were holding the world together, the way the world needs to be held together. There is even a tone of benignity to the voice of becalmed whiteness. A working voice, a hum of productivity. The world as its material. The voice of whiteness extracts maximal value from this material. The voice of whiteness, the beast of whiteness, is the voice and the beast first of extraction and then, when finished with that, the voice of elimination.

There is scant sign of idiosyncrasy in this voice. No matter that it may be rooted in our most private, urgent experiences of unmet desire, its targeted objects are entirely standardized. The prescribed ideas, attitudes, and inclinations to be adopted toward these standardized objects of hatred also lack originality. These objects are self-evidently dangerous, and the appropriate sentiments and behaviors, no matter how violent, all share the

D. Hook, *Whiteness at the Abyss*, The Palgrave Lacan Series,
https://doi.org/10.1007/978-3-031-78509-2

stated aim of promoting safety and diminishing threat. Knowledge of the hated objects' noxious qualities and of the prescriptions and proscriptions related to their proper handling are felt to be derived from sources that both pre-date and supersede any particular experience. The primary function of any personal experience with the objects in question is neither the discovery nor the generation of new ideas and affects, but rather the gathering of confirmatory evidence. With such evidence in hand, people can tap into what feels like the wisdom of the ancients. This wisdom is codified into systems of belief, structures of knowledge linked to a taxonomy, an organizing notion that the human world is, at bedrock, made up of hierarchically arranged groups.

What happens, then, when the voice of whiteness as white supremacy, gets called out? Gets named as an imposter, gets challenged, gets reduced? What happens when its predations are re-framed, more the actions of willful criminality, now, than of natural appetite? No longer a grizzly bear but instead a fragile human costumed as a grizzly bear? What happens when the costume gets more of our attention than do the teeth and the claws? Does the voice of whiteness then still maintain itself as a single organism, or does it disintegrate into multiple voices, each one now claiming its own idiosyncratic perspective?

Like Derek Hook, I have worked on the costumes worn by whiteness' voice of white supremacy. And consequently, like Derek, I have been targeted by the voice of 'outraged whiteness'. Derek and I have each preserved some of the targeting messages we've received. We do not write to identical audiences. We do not share identical theorizations. What we do share is a certainty that whiteness, when it goes malignant, warrants muscular scrutiny and vigilant opposition. But first of all, its pretenses warrant exposure. And what we have now found—Derek and I—is that when those pretenses are exposed, white supremacist 'whiteness' becomes outraged. No surprise there. What is at least moderately surprising, though, is that the voice of outraged whiteness is as standardized and formulaic as its voice of naturalized predation.

Essentially, Derek and I received identical messages—identical. Nothing distinguishes his from mine. See 'his' in Chap. 4 and you are also seeing mine from the aftermath of 'On Having Whiteness' (Moss, 2021).

In reflecting on these messages, Derek writes that it would be hard to believe that the senders were 'convinced' of much of what they sent: that he was a Jew Commie Bolshevik Nazi Suicidal Genocidal Hyper-Woke Intellectual Pervert, etc. (We might as well treat this list as one compound word.) The same notion of one single compound word might hold were we to ask the senders to speak to us of their certainties regarding people of color: we know in advance all the attributes about which they will be certain. I do not think the senders are ever 'convinced' of what they transmit, whether the transmission comes from either a becalmed or outraged condition.

Either way, I think the senders proceed not by way of conviction but rather by way of revelation. White supremacy, whether becalmed or outraged, totally bypasses the tentativeness of first-hand experience and inference. It arrives at knowledge whole-hog and entire. In effect, the voices of white supremacy give direct expression to what they might call a **miracle.** Miraculously, they are the apex predators. Miraculously, they are entitled without limit. Miraculously, they are beyond the reach of regulation and law. And miraculously, they are, indeed, the world's supreme lawmakers. And we, who might not believe in white supremacy's founding miracle, well, we are, then, defilers. And I think that's the proper word for us: defilers. We defile, we pollute, we infect, we diminish, we destroy. For the outraged voice of white supremacy, we are infidels. We have betrayed the miraculous gift they offer us. This, I think, accounts for how often Derek and I were each targeted as 'Jews', 'kikes', etc. ... Those whose constitutions not only prevent them from recognizing the miracle before them, but also lead them toward ruining, even 'killing' off the people of the miracle—the white supremacists. And as such, we 'Jews' warrant elimination.

....

No matter how daunting the ferocity and power of white supremacy's apex predators, we psychoanalysts must claim our place at the table. And to do so, we must be able to think clinically, treating white supremacy as a perverse symptom, deeply sited in individuals and in the social surround. As a symptom, then, we can proceed with confidence that white supremacy has its determinants, that it is not essential, that it emerges, and that therefore it can be dismantled.

The moment we think of the voice of white supremacy as emerging from the imagined position of an apex predator, we realize that this predation is grounded in the vision of a world structured vertically. 'Apex' is the giveaway term. Verticality is the social and psychic precondition that provides host receptor sites for white supremacist ideas. Vertical structures abound, both psychically and socially. The social ones are so abundant as to not require naming here. As for the psychic ones: Think of the ego's efforts at 'mastering' drive demands. Think of the superego's efforts to regulate and control. Think of narcissistic states of mind and their associated grandiosities. Think of the border separating self from other—pleasure here (inside), pain there (outside).

Along each of these vertical planes, object relations—internal and external—are defined by power and grounded in fantasies of sovereignty—the final elimination of conflict. We are all tentatively located somewhere along each of these multiple planes—tentative because we are always aware of the possibility of falling. This vertical fragility makes us all susceptible. White supremacy's voice caresses its hosts with reassurances; never again, it can seem to murmur, will you have to be alone. An always strained and always jeopardized 'I am' will necessarily be susceptible to this pre-formed dream of an always empowered 'We are'.

The key point here is that white supremacist ideas need a host in order to survive. Psychoanalytically informed treatments, then, of individual patients or of susceptible groups, need not address those ideas directly. Instead, and in fact more fundamentally, such treatments may target verticality itself, in all of its expressions. Verticality depends upon disidentification. I am not whatever is above or below me. Diminish disidentifications and you necessarily diminish verticality's skeleton. Identifications, looking for and finding likeness—this is the central clinical, and social, move that undermines verticality, and therefore can turn fixed hierarchy into mobile difference.

Reference

Moss, D. (2021). On having Whiteness. *Journal of the American Psychoanalytical Association, 69*(2), 355–371.

Coda: Suicide as an Emancipatory Political Act[1]

Slavoj Žižek

Can we imagine a successful suicide as an emancipatory political act? The first association here is of course public suicides as a protest against foreign occupation, from Vietnam to Poland in the 1980s. In the last years, however, a suicidal proposal aroused a wide debate in South Africa. Derek Hook reports how, in March 2016, Terblanche Delport, a young white academic, sparked outrage at a Johannesburg conference at the University of the Witwatersrand, when he called on white people in South Africa "to commit suicide as an ethical act"—here are Delport's own words:

> The reality [in South Africa] is that most white people spend their whole lives only engaging black people in subservient positions – cleaners, gardeners, etc. My question is then how can a person not be racist if that's the way they live their lives? The only way then for white people to become part of Africa is to not exist as white people anymore. If the goal is to dismantle white supremacy, and white supremacy is white culture and vice versa, then the goal has to be to dismantle white culture and ultimately white people themselves. The total integration into Africa by white people will also automatically then mean the death of white people as white as a concept would not exist anymore. (Delport, cited in Hook, 2020, p. 613)

How, more concretely, are we to imagine the symbolic suicide of the South African Whites? Donald Moss proposed a simple but problematic

D. Hook, *Whiteness at the Abyss*, The Palgrave Lacan Series,
https://doi.org/10.1007/978-3-031-78509-2

(for me, at least) solution: the racist Whiteness is a parasitic formation which parasitizes on Whites themselves:

> Whiteness is a condition one first acquires and then one has—a malignant, parasitic-like condition to which "white" people have a particular susceptibility. The condition is foundational, generating characteristic ways of being in one's body, in one's mind, and in one's world. Parasitic Whiteness renders its hosts' appetites voracious, insatiable, and perverse. These deformed appetites particularly target nonwhite peoples. Once established, these appetites are nearly impossible to eliminate. (Moss, 2021, p. 355)

To get rid of their racist stance, the whites have to get rid of the parasitic whiteness which is not part of their substantial nature but just parasitizes on them, which means that, in getting rid of their racism, they do not lose the substance of their being—they even regain it, obliterating its distortion ... I prefer to this easy way out Hook's comment (inspired by Lacanian theory):

> Delport's rhetorical and deliberately provocative suggestion is perhaps not as counter-intuitive or crazy as it at first sounds. Arguably, it is the gesture of giving up what one is – the shedding of narcissistic investments, and symbolic and fantasmatic identities – that proves a necessary first step to becoming what one is not, but might become. This is the transformative potential of anxiety that clinicians work so hard to facilitate and that I think can also be discerned – however fleetingly – in the instances of white anxiety discussed above: the potentiality that a new – and hitherto unthinkable – form of identification is being unconsciously processed and negotiated. (Hook, 2020, p. 628)

What I nonetheless find problematic in these lines is the optimist turn: suicide does not mean the actual collective self-killing of the South African whites, it means a symbolic erasure of their identity which already points toward new forms of identity ... I find it much more productive to establish a link between this idea of the whites' collective suicide and the idea of so-called afro-pessimism. Recall Fanon's claim that the Negro is "a zone of non-being, an extraordinarily sterile and arid region, an utterly declining declivity" (2008, p. 2): is the experience that grounds today's "afro-pessimism" not a similar one? Does the insistence of afro-pessimists that Black subordination is much more radical than that of other underprivileged groups (Asians, LGBT+, women ...), i.e., that Blacks should not be put into the series with other forms of "colonization," not grounded in the act of assuming that one belongs to such a "zone of nonbeing"? This is why Fredric Jameson is right when he insists that one cannot understand class struggle in the US without taking into account anti-Black racism: any talk which equalizes white and Black proletarians is a fake. (A point to be noted here is that, when the young Gandhi protested against the white rule in South Africa, he ignored the plight of the Black majority and just demanded the inclusion of Indians into the privileged White block.) So, what if we turn Delport's suggestion, radical as it may appear, around and propose that it is the Blacks in South Africa who should commit a collective symbolic suicide, to shed their socio-symbolic identity which is profoundly marked by white domination and resistance to it, and which contains its own fantasies and even narcissistic investments of victimization?

Consequently, I see afro-pessimism not just as a recognition of dismal social reality but also and above all as something that announces "the potentiality that a new—and hitherto unthinkable—form of identification is being unconsciously processed and negotiated." To put it brutally, let's imagine that, in one way or another, all the Whites would disappear from South Africa—the ANC inefficiency and corruption would remain, and the poor black majority would find itself even more strongly dislocated, lacking the designated cause of its poverty ... To revolutionize a system is never equal to just eliminating one of its parts, in the same way that the disappearance of Jews as the disturbing element never restores social harmony. The key move has to be done by Blacks themselves—was Malcolm X not following this insight when he adopted X as his family name? The point of choosing X as his family name and thereby signaling that the slave traders who brought the enslaved Africans from their homeland brutally deprived them of their family and ethnic roots, of their entire cultural life-world, was not to mobilize the blacks to fight for the return to some primordial African roots, but precisely to seize the opening provided by X, an unknown new (lack of) identity engendered by the very process of slavery which made the African roots forever lost. The idea is that this X which deprives the blacks of their particular tradition offers a unique chance to redefine (reinvent) themselves, to freely form a new identity much more universal than white people's professed universality. (As is well known, Malcolm X found this new identity in the universalism of Islam.) To put it in Hook's terms, Malcolm X proposes for Blacks themselves to bring to the end their deracination with a gesture of symbolic suicide, the passage through zero-point, in order to free the space for a new identity. Such a gesture would render the White domination simply pointless, a solipsist dream, a game missing a partner with whom it can only be played.

Note

1. In 2022, Slavoj Žižek published an article entitled 'Three fragments on suicide as a political factor' in the journal *Crisis & Critique*. One section of that article was focused on my psychoanalytic discussion of white anxiety and related notions of suicide. Slavoj, and the editors of the journal, were kind enough to give their permission for that section of commentary to be reproduced here.

References

Fanon, F. (2008). *Black Skin White Masks* (C. L. Markmann, Trans.). Pluto.

Hook, D. (2020). White anxiety in (post)apartheid South Africa. *Psychoanalysis, Culture and Society, 25*, 612–631.

Moss, D. (2021). On having Whiteness. *Journal of the American Psychoanalytical Association, 69*(2), 355–371.

Žižek, S. (2022). Three fragments on suicide as a political factor. *Crisis & Critique, 9*(2), 414–425.

Index[1]

A

B

[1] Note: Page numbers followed by 'n' refer to notes.

D. Hook, *Whiteness at the Abyss*, The Palgrave Lacan Series,
https://doi.org/10.1007/978-3-031-78509-2

R

S

T

U

The manufacturer's authorised representative in the EU is Springer Nature Customer Service Centre GmbH, Europaplatz 3, 69115 Heidelberg, Germany. If you have any concerns regarding our products, please contact ProductSafety@springernature.com

Printed and bound by CPI Group (UK) Ltd, Croydon, CR0 4YY
01/10/2026
02225978-0005